Emotional Alchemy: Transforming Feelings into Personal Growth

A Practical Handbook for Emotional Intelligence

Ethan Harrison

Table of Contents

INTRODUCTION

Welcome to "Emotional Alchemy: Transforming Feelings into Personal Growth," a practical handbook designed to guide you on a transformative journey toward emotional intelligence. In the intricate landscape of our emotions lies the key to personal growth and self-discovery. This book serves as a compass, offering valuable insights and actionable strategies to harness the power of emotional alchemy.

In the fast-paced and complex world we navigate daily, emotional intelligence has emerged as a crucial skill. Understanding and managing our emotions not only enhances our well-being but also paves the way for meaningful personal development. This handbook is more than just a collection of theories; it is a roadmap for turning your emotional experiences into catalysts for growth.

The concept of emotional alchemy is rooted in the idea that, like an alchemist transforms base metals into gold, we can transform challenging emotions into opportunities for self-discovery and positive change. This process involves understanding the intricate nuances of our emotions, developing the skills to regulate them, and using their energy to fuel personal growth.

Throughout this journey, we will explore the fundamental components of emotional intelligence, delving into the art of recognizing and regulating emotions. Practical exercises and techniques will empower you to navigate the complexities of your emotional landscape, fostering resilience and cultivating positive emotional well-being.

Whether you are seeking to enhance your professional success, build healthier relationships, or simply embark on a path of self-discovery, this handbook provides the tools and guidance to help you navigate the transformative process of emotional alchemy. Let us embark on this journey together, as we unlock the secrets of Emotional Alchemy and turn the raw materials of our feelings into the gold of personal growth.

CHAPTER I

Understanding Emotional Alchemy

Definition and Concept

The concept of Emotional Alchemy is a profound exploration into the transformative power of emotions, offering a unique lens through which individuals can approach personal growth. In its most fundamental form, emotional alchemy can be understood as a complex process that involves transforming the raw materials of human emotions into beneficial insights and possibilities for coming to terms with oneself. The historical idea of alchemy, in which practitioners attempted to transmute base metals into gold, is a source of inspiration for this voyage of transformation through history. The analogies are remarkable in the arena of feelings; emotional alchemy aims to transform complex sentiments into the precious metal of personal growth.

The underlying premise that underpins the practice of emotional alchemy is that feelings are not only temporary sensations but rather powerful forces that may be harnessed and directed toward positive change. In contrast to conventional perspectives, which classify feelings as positive or negative, emotional alchemy acknowledges the complex and diverse nature of human emotions. All of the feelings we experience, whether happiness, sadness, rage, or fear, are regarded as valuable components of the alchemical process because they can bring about personal development and understanding.

A profound comprehension of feelings is the first step on the alchemical path. This involves going beyond surface-level reactions and investigating the deeper meanings and triggers beneath them. Individuals' increased emotional awareness is a fundamental component of the process because it enables them to navigate the landscapes within themselves with more clarity. Deciphering the transforming power of emotions requires an acknowledgment of the complexities and diversity of these feelings.

The concept of emotional intelligence is essential to the practice of dynamic alchemy. Emotional intelligence refers to the capacity to identify, comprehend, and control one's feelings, as well as the capacity to sympathize with the feelings of others. The alchemical voyage is a journey that requires emotional intelligence to act as the guiding compass, offering the skills needed to navigate the ebb and flow of emotions. As individuals work to improve their emotional intelligence, they become more adept at shifting emotional obstacles into opportunities for personal development.

To complete the alchemical process, one must have a visceral involvement with one's emotional experiences. This is in addition to having a superficial intellectual grasp of emotions. The purpose of this engagement is not to repress or dismiss feelings; instead, it is to acknowledge them in their entirety and to accept the importance of the lessons they convey. When people do this, they go on a journey of self-discovery, which involves peeling back layers of conditioned responses and cultural expectations to unveil their true selves.

The development of tools for emotional regulation is an essential component of the spiritual practice known as emotional alchemy. Individuals are given the ability to navigate the strength of their emotions and constructively channel their energy by utilizing these procedures for alchemical purposes. The alchemist's toolkit should include vital components such as breathing exercises, mindfulness practices, and other ways. These methods provide a practical means of transforming emotional obstacles into chances for growth.

Transforming what is commonly referred to as "negative" emotions is one of the fundamental foundations of emotional alchemy. Instead of considering negative emotions such as grief, anger, or fear as obstacles to one's well-being, emotional alchemy encourages individuals to investigate the alchemical processes that can transform these feelings into beneficial understandings. Individuals can learn from their experiences by recasting the narrative around complicated feelings. This allows them to unearth previously concealed pieces of themselves and cultivate resilience in the face of hardship.

Furthermore, the use of Emotional Alchemy extends beyond the confines of the individual, finding use in places such as professional settings and interpersonal connections. When it comes to interpersonal connections, the alchemical approach fosters feelings of empathy and compassion and encourages efficient communication. Individuals can establish healthier friendships and navigate disagreements more easily if they are better aware of the emotional dynamics at play. Regarding effective leadership in the workplace, emotional intelligence becomes an essential component. This involves the creation of conditions that encourage cooperation, innovation, and the overall well-being of employees.

In addition, emotional alchemy has significant repercussions on how future generations are brought up. Considering the significance of early dynamic education, the alchemical method promotes the idea that children should be taught emotional intelligence right from the start. Society can create the groundwork for a more emotionally resilient and empathic future if it provides young minds with the tools necessary to navigate their emotions.

Individuals engage on a never-ending path of personal development as they go through the process of incorporating Emotional Alchemy into their day-to-day lives. By transforming challenges into opportunities and failures into catalysts for transformation, the alchemical processes become engrained in their approach to overcoming challenges. The handbook, "Emotional Alchemy: Transforming Feelings into Personal Growth," acts as a comprehensive guide on this journey. It provides individuals with practical exercises, insights, and tools to support their pursuit of emotional intelligence and alchemical self-discovery.

In conclusion, Emotional Alchemy is a paradigm change in how we perceive and interact with our feelings and emotions. Instead, it is an invitation to investigate the complexity and depth of our emotional experiences, with the understanding that these experiences are crucial components in the grand alchemy of personal development. Individuals can negotiate the intricacies of their inner worlds by embracing the principles of emotional intelligence and alchemical transformation. This allows them to change the raw materials of their feelings into the gold of self-awareness, resilience, and authentic life.

Historical Perspectives on Emotional Alchemy

The practice of alchemy, an ancient method that aimed to change base metals into gold, served as the source of inspiration for the development of emotional alchemy, which originates in the annals of history. While it is true that the alchemists of the past may have concentrated on the material world, to this day, it is impossible to deny the similarities between their endeavors and the contemporary idea of emotional alchemy. To acquire an understanding of the historical underpinnings of Emotional Alchemy, it is necessary to investigate the development of alchemy itself and the symbolic resonance that it possesses in a variety of civilizations.

As an esoteric tradition, alchemy flourished throughout a variety of civilizations at the same time, including ancient Egypt, China, Greece, and the Islamic world. In ancient societies, alchemists were not only interested in the transformation of material in a physical sense, but they also aimed to achieve spiritual enlightenment and the perfection of the human soul. It is believed that the philosopher's stone, a legendary material supposed to facilitate the transformation of base metals into gold, became a symbol for the alchemical quest, representing the alchemist's journey as they undertook a transformational process.

Alchemy flourished as a multidimensional study throughout the Islamic Golden Age. It included elements of philosophy, mysticism, and proto-science. Scholars such as Jabir ibn Hayyan made substantial contributions to the literature of alchemy, thereby providing the framework for symbolic and practical alchemy. By the more expansive spiritual objectives of alchemy, the transformation of metals was regarded as a material process and a method of cleaning the soul.

As alchemy spread westward, it became more prominent in medieval Europe, where practitioners such as Paracelsus contributed to the development of the practice. Alchemical ideas were incorporated into Paracelsus's medical philosophy, which is another reason why he is widely considered the father of modern chemistry. He strongly emphasized the concept of a "universal medicine" that can heal both the bodily and spiritual parts of a human, respectively. The alchemical idea of the interdependence of the material and spiritual realms was mirrored in this holistic approach to well-being, which followed the same principles.

As the practice of alchemy developed, its symbolism got more complex, and symbolic storylines gradually captured the imagination of those who engaged in the practice. It was common practice to show the alchemical process as a progression of stages, which included calcination, dissolution, coagulation, and the elusive confluence. These stages represented the disintegration and reconstruction of the self on both the physical and metaphysical levels, which reflected the transformational journey that the alchemist underwent.

In the context of emotional alchemy, the historical roots can be traced back to the realization of the alchemists that the transformational process extends beyond the realm of the outward world and into the realm of the mind. Emotional Alchemy uses the metaphorical language of alchemy to explain the inner transformation of emotions. This transformation involves transforming human sentiments' fundamental, raw elements into the precious gold of personal development and self-awareness.

During the Renaissance, there was a resurgence of interest in alchemy, brought about by individuals such as Marsilio Ficino and the Hermetic revivalists who investigated the mystical components of the practice. With its emphasis on the oneness of the spiritual and material worlds, the Hermetic tradition offered a fertile environment for integrating emotional and spiritual alchemy. This was because the Hermetic tradition encouraged the union of the two realms.

Moving forward to the present day, the idea of emotional alchemy has emerged as a modern interpretation of the ancient wisdom passed down through the generations. The symbolic resonance of alchemy, which focuses on transformation and the search for inner gold, discovers a new relevance in investigating emotions as catalysts for personal development. Tara Bennett-Goleman, a psychotherapist, is credited with popularizing "emotional alchemy." In her book "Emotional Alchemy: How the Mind Can Heal the Heart," she incorporated mindfulness and cognitive therapy with emotional transmutation, an ancient tradition.

In a historical framework, emotional alchemy can be understood as a natural extension of the alchemical heritage, adapting its principles to the challenges and opportunities of the modern psychological terrain. This has been the case since the beginning of the practice. In the furnace of the alchemist's laboratory or the crucible of the human heart and intellect, the historical perspectives on emotional alchemy highlight the everlasting quest for transformation. This journey can take place in either setting.

In addition, the symbolic language of alchemy offers a rich tapestry that can be utilized for comprehending the intricacies of feelings. There is a parallel between the emotional processes of self-discovery and personal progress and the alchemical stages, including the ego's disintegration, the integration of antagonistic energies, and the breaking down of old structures. Through embracing this historical continuum, Emotional Alchemy encourages individuals to go on an inner alchemical journey to transform the fundamental feelings experienced in daily life into the precious gold of self-awareness and resilience.

In conclusion, the historical perspectives on emotional alchemy reveal a fascinating journey through the corridors of time, where the alchemists of old tried not only to convert metals but also to unravel the mysteries of the human soul. This voyage revealed an exciting journey through the corridors of time. Emotional Alchemy, which originates in this historical tapestry, gives ancient knowledge a new lease on life by encouraging individuals to interact with their feelings as if they were performing alchemical transformations in their existence. While exploring the historical repercussions of alchemy, we realize that the alchemical drive for transformation is not limited to a particular era. Instead, it has found a contemporary manifestation in the profound journey of emotional alchemy.

The Role of Emotional Alchemy in Modern Psychology

Within the ever-evolving field of psychology, the combination of old knowledge and modern ideas has developed novel ways to address the intricacies of human emotions. A notion that originates in the historical tradition of alchemy but has been adapted to the context of emotional well-being and personal development is known as emotional alchemy. This approach has acquired popularity in contemporary psychology and is one of the approaches that has gained traction. An investigation into the principles and applications of emotional alchemy, as well as how it contributes to our comprehension and control of emotions, is necessary to understand the function that emotional alchemy plays in contemporary psychology.

Traditional paradigms, which frequently regard emotions as either positive or negative, are challenged by Emotional Alchemy, which, at its core, marks a departure from these beliefs. As an alternative, it accepts that every emotion can transform, analogous to the alchemical process of transforming base metals into gold. The usual dichotomy of positive and negative emotions is called into question by this paradigm shift, which encourages individuals to investigate the extensiveness and richness of their emotional experiences without passing judgment on them.

Modern psychology recognizes the complex relationship between cognition and emotion, and the concept of emotional alchemy provides a fresh perspective through which to investigate this connection. In Emotional Alchemy, cognitive restructuring is combined with the principles of transformation derived from alchemy. This approach draws inspiration from cognitive-behavioral therapy (CBT) and mindfulness practices. Like cognitive-behavioral therapists, practitioners of emotional alchemy urge patients to recognize and challenge harmful thought patterns. At the same time, they emphasize the transforming potential that is inherent in emotional experiences.

In addition, Emotional Alchemy is congruent with the rapidly developing discipline of positive psychology, which is centered on cultivating strengths, virtues, and total well-being. Rather than focusing solely on reducing suffering, the positive psychology movement emphasizes the significance of flourishing. The program Emotional Alchemy contributes to this paradigm by offering tools that help people manage negative emotions and actively transform them into sources of personal development. Emotional Alchemy is consistent with the objective of positive psychology, which is to increase the overall level of satisfaction and fulfillment that individuals experience in their lives.

A lot of recognition in contemporary psychological interventions has been given to mindfulness, a fundamental component of emotional alchemy. Mindfulness is an essential component in the method of emotional regulation that Emotional Alchemy utilizes. Mindfulness is defined as the practice of paying attention to the present moment without passing judgment on your experience. Through mindfulness, individuals can learn to notice their feelings with a heightened awareness, enabling them to respond to stressful situations with clarity and serenity. Emotional Alchemy's significance in addressing contemporary challenges linked to stress, anxiety, and overall mental well-being is highlighted by the incorporation of mindfulness practices into the treatment.

There is also a connection between the study of existential psychology and the field of emotional alchemy. Existential psychology investigates the human experience of meaning, choice, and responsibility. Existential psychology strongly emphasizes the significance of tackling existential problems, such as the fear of death and the desire for purpose in one's life.

This perspective is aligned with the Emotional Alchemy approach, which encourages individuals to address and overcome existential worries via the alchemical processes of acceptance and personal development. In engaging in Emotional Alchemy, individuals start on a path of self-discovery and purposeful life by confronting the depths of their emotional experiences.

In addition to addressing the well-being of individuals, the therapeutic applications of emotional alchemy extend into the sphere of interpersonal interactions. This book, Emotional Alchemy, provides insights into effective communication, conflict resolution, and the cultivation of empathy. It does this by acknowledging the impact of emotions on the dynamics of social relationships. Individuals benefit from the alchemical approach because it teaches them to comprehend not only their feelings but also the feelings that other people are experiencing. This increased emotional intelligence becomes vital in developing more robust connections and resolving interpersonal issues, contributing to the expanding field of relationship-focused therapies.

Within the field of trauma-informed care, Emotional Alchemy offers a framework that enables individuals to negotiate and transcend traumatic events while also supporting them. It is common for catastrophic experiences to leave an indelible mark on an individual's emotional well-being, and Emotional Alchemy recognizes the significant impact that traumatic events may have. Through the perspective of alchemy, individuals are helped to investigate the transforming potential within their traumatic experiences, reframing their narratives and reclaiming agency over their emotional responses. Taking this approach is consistent with contemporary trauma therapies, which emphasize empowering individuals and building resilience in the face of tragedy.

As the field of psychology evolves to embrace a more holistic perspective of mental health, the mind-body connection has emerged as a central focus of research and intervention. Through the recognition of the bodily side of emotions, which refers to how emotions appear in the body, Emotional Alchemy contributes to this perspective. Emotional Alchemy is a concept that integrates elements from somatic psychology and emphasizes the significance of embodied awareness in the process of emotional transformation. A holistic approach to emotional well-being can be fostered through techniques such as breathwork, movement, and body-centered mindfulness, which become vital tools in the toolset of an alchemist.

Within the realm of education, the ideas of Emotional Alchemy are utilized in the rapidly developing discipline of social-emotional learning (SEL), a subfield of education. Social and emotional learning (SEL) programs provide students with the tools necessary to comprehend and control their feelings, create meaningful relationships, and make responsible choices. By highlighting the transformative potential within emotional experiences, Emotional Alchemy offers a framework complementary to Social and Emotional Learning (SEL). Educators significantly contribute to developing emotionally intelligent and resilient individuals by introducing pupils to the alchemical processes of self-awareness and emotional control.

The incorporation of technology into interventions for mental health has emerged as a defining characteristic of contemporary psychology. This movement is aligned with Emotional Alchemy, which uses internet platforms to share materials, tools, and guided practices. Mobile applications, virtual therapy sessions, and online groups that are dedicated to emotional alchemy are all accessible routes that allow individuals to participate in the transforming processes without having to leave the comfort of their environs. The potential of Emotional Alchemy to adapt to new circumstances and remain relevant in the present era is demonstrated by the combination of contemporary technology with traditional knowledge.

To summarize, the role of emotional alchemy in contemporary psychology is multifaceted. It encompasses various concepts and practices, including cognitive-behavioral principles, positive psychology, mindfulness practices, existential considerations, trauma-informed care, relationship-focused therapies, somatic psychology, and educational interventions. As an approach to emotions that is both holistic and transformative, Emotional Alchemy resonates with the changing landscape of psychology. It provides individuals and practitioners with a comprehensive framework that can be used to traverse the intricacies of the human experience. Emotional alchemy emerges as a vital ally in pursuing emotional well-being, personal progress, and achieving human potential. This is accomplished by merging ancient wisdom with contemporary discoveries.

CHAPTER II

The Basics of Emotional Intelligence

Definition and Components of Emotional Intelligence

Emotional intelligence, often abbreviated as EQ, has emerged as a pivotal concept in psychology, influencing personal development, interpersonal relationships, and professional success. In the early 1990s, psychologists Peter Salovey and John D. Mayer were the ones who first popularized the phrase "emotional intelligence." Subsequently, "emotional intelligence" garnered wider prominence due to the innovative work of novelist and psychologist Daniel Goleman. Emotional intelligence can be broken down into its fundamental components, which include the capacity to detect, comprehend, control, and make efficient use of one's feelings, as well as the ability to perceive and affect the feelings of other people. To successfully navigate the complexities of human interactions, it is essential to have emotional awareness and the ability to regulate it. This comprehensive skill set goes beyond traditional measurements of intelligence, such as IQ.

Emotional intelligence may be broken down into several important aspects, each of which significantly determines an individual's overall emotional intelligence. These dimensions can be defined as the components of emotional intelligence. The ability to recognize and comprehend one's feelings is an essential component of self-awareness, one of the fundamental aspects. A precondition for developing other elements of emotional intelligence is the ability to engage in introspection, which serves as the basis of emotional intelligence. People with a high level of self-awareness can identify their emotional states effectively, understand the reasons behind their feelings, and know how their emotions may impact their thoughts and behaviors.

In addition to being an essential component of emotional intelligence, self-regulation is also vital. A person's capacity to properly manage and control their emotions is the focus of this aspect of the personality. If an individual possesses good self-regulation skills, they can maneuver through difficult situations without being overcome by negative emotions. Individuals with this talent for emotional resilience can keep their composure, make judgments that are in their best interests, and adjust to constantly shifting situations. In addition, self-regulation entails the ability to defer gratification and resist impulsive impulses, which contribute to achieving long-term professional goals.

One of the most critical aspects of emotional intelligence is empathy, which is frequently considered the foundation of social intelligence. The capacity to comprehend and share other people's emotions is an essential component of empathy, which helps to cultivate more robust connections and a better understanding of interpersonal dynamics. Individuals who possess high levels of empathy can tune into the emotional states of those around them, which facilitates successful communication, the settlement of conflicts, and the implementation of collaborative activities. The ability of those who are empathic to perceive the emotional experiences of others is enhanced by their sensitivity to non-verbal clues, such as body language and facial expressions.

The ability to skillfully traverse social dynamics is inextricably linked to developing interpersonal connections, an essential component of emotional intelligence. Effective communication, the ability to resolve conflicts, and the capacity to create and sustain strong relationships are all included in this dimension. People who can develop relationships with others, communicate confidently, and negotiate the complexities of group dynamics are individuals who have excellent interpersonal skills. Not only does the ability to form meaningful relationships help one's emotional well- being, but it also contributes to one's professional success because it encourages effective leadership and teamwork development.

The capacity to control one's feelings to initiate and maintain motivation is at the heart of the concept of motivation, which is a component of emotional intelligence. Intrinsic motivation is a form that goes beyond the pursuit of external benefits and encompasses a strong desire to achieve personal and professional objectives. Motivated individuals will demonstrate resilience in the face of failures, keep an optimistic view, and persevere in their efforts to attain success. There is a strong connection between this aspect of emotional intelligence and the notion of self-determination, which emphasizes the significance of autonomy, competence, and relatedness in cultivating intrinsic drive.

In conclusion, social skills are the final component of emotional intelligence. These skills comprise a wide range of qualities relevant to successful interactions with other people. Socially skilled people can negotiate various social circumstances, communicate compellingly, and construct networks that facilitate collaboration. In addition to positively influencing and inspiring others, these abilities include sharing effectively and resolving conflicts. Socially adept individuals perform exceptionally well in group settings, whether participating in the workplace, the community, or personal relationships. They contribute to a social environment that is peaceful and supportive.

Many facets of life are significantly impacted by emotional intelligence, including personal and professional spheres. Emotional intelligence is comprised of a wide range of components. At educational institutions, developing emotional intelligence helps create an atmosphere that is constructive and encouraging for students to learn. Students who possess a high level of emotional intelligence can defuse stressful situations, successfully traverse social hurdles, and effectively communicate with their classmates and teachers. Programs that combine the development of emotional intelligence are beneficial to the educational environment because they build well-rounded individuals capable of navigating the difficulties of the academic path.

These days, emotional intelligence is one of the most critical factors determining workplace success. The benefit of individuals who possess technical skills and display emotional intelligence in their interactions is becoming increasingly recognized by employers. A high level of emotional intelligence helps cultivate successful leadership, teamwork, and communication, which improves the culture of a business and its overall productivity. Leaders with high emotional intelligence can inspire and encourage their colleagues, cultivate a healthy work environment, and overcome problems with resilience.

Regarding mental health, emotional intelligence is a significant factor in helping individuals comprehend and take control of their emotional well-being. Individuals who possess a high level of emotional intelligence are better suited to deal with psychological obstacles such as stress, anxiety, and other mental health issues. They can control their feelings, seek assistance when required, and participate in healthy coping mechanisms that are adaptive to their circumstances. When individuals get therapeutic interventions that incorporate the principles of emotional intelligence, they are provided with tools that can help them improve their emotional well-being and resilience more effectively.

In the global and cultural understanding framework, emotional intelligence is also significant and significant in its own right. Communication and understanding across cultures require a high level of emotional intelligence to successfully negotiate the many viewpoints, conventions, and communication styles among different cultures. People with a high level of emotional intelligence can bridge cultural divides, recognize and manage cultural nuances, and establish meaningful connections with people from various backgrounds. In today's linked and diverse world, the ability to empathize with people of different cultures is becoming increasingly appreciated.

Emotional intelligence is a multidimensional skill set that influences numerous human connection and well-being areas. In conclusion, emotional intelligence and its components contain many potential outcomes. Each component that contributes to the formation of an individual's overall emotional intelligence plays a significant role in the process. These components include self-awareness, self-regulation, empathy, interpersonal interactions, motivation, and social skills. As the relevance of emotional intelligence in both personal and professional success continues to be recognized by society, the cultivation of these talents becomes a personal quest and a community activity to create a more emotionally intelligent and empathic world.

The Four Branches of Emotional Intelligence

The concept of emotional intelligence, as popularized by psychologists Peter Salovey and John D. Mayer and later expanded upon by Daniel Goleman, is multifaceted, comprising four distinct branches that collectively shape an individual's emotional intelligence profile. These four facets, namely self-awareness, self-regulation, social awareness, and relationship management, constitute the structure that serves as the basis for comprehending and improving emotional intelligence.

The ability to perceive and comprehend one's feelings is the first component of emotional intelligence: self-awareness. Because it is the foundation upon which other aspects of emotional intelligence are constructed, this ability to engage in self-reflection is essential to being emotionally intelligent. People with a high level of self-awareness can identify their emotional states effectively, understand the reasons behind their feelings, and know how their emotions may impact their thoughts and behaviors. Individuals can better understand their strengths, limitations, and areas for personal improvement when they have the capacity for self- reflection. A more genuine connection with oneself and the development of emotional resilience are outcomes of cultivating self-awareness, which involves not only the recognition of pleasant emotions but also the acknowledgment and resolution of negative emotions.

Both self-awareness and self-regulation are components of emotional intelligence, the second branch of emotional intelligence. Acquiring the skill of efficiently managing and controlling one's emotions is necessary. If an individual possesses good self-regulation skills, they can maneuver through difficult situations without being overcome by negative emotions. Individuals who possess this talent for emotional resilience can keep their composure, make judgments that are in their best interests, and adjust to constantly shifting situations. In addition, self-regulation entails the ability to defer gratification and resist impulsive impulses, which contribute to achieving long-term professional goals. In its most basic form, self-regulation refers to preserving emotional equilibrium and refraining from allowing overwhelming feelings to govern one's actions. This ultimately results in reactions that are more thoughtful and sensible to life's problems.

The third subfield of emotional intelligence is known as social awareness, and it is concentrated on the ability to recognize and comprehend the feelings that different people are experiencing. Individuals must be able to tune into the emotional states of those around them to develop this aspect of emotional intelligence, which goes beyond individual introspection. Individuals with a high level of social awareness can sympathize with other people, interpret non-verbal clues, and understand the impact that a particular circumstance has on their emotions. Possessing this ability to successfully navigate interpersonal interactions, cultivate effective communication, and establish rapport is essential. Individuals who are socially aware can interpret subtle social cues, allowing them to modify their conduct to meet the emotional requirements of various settings and cultivate a heightened sensitivity to other people's feelings.

The fourth subfield of emotional intelligence is known as relationship management, and it comprises a wide range of skills associated with successful interactions with other people. This aspect extends beyond simply being able to recognize and comprehend feelings; it also entails using this comprehension to construct and sustain positive connections. The ability to communicate assertively, resolve issues politely, and traverse the complexity of group dynamics are all qualities that individuals with good relationship management skills possess. The ability to inspire and motivate others, form collaborative networks, and create a good work atmosphere are all essential components of effective leadership, which is why this particular aspect of emotional intelligence is vital in organizational leadership jobs. Relationship management requires interpersonal skills and the capacity to influence and inspire other people favorably, which helps to cultivate a feeling of shared purpose and collective accomplishment.

A person's overall emotional well-being and success in various life domains are influenced by these four subfields of emotional intelligence, which are interrelated and contribute to the individual's emotional well-being together. The importance of taking a comprehensive approach to the development of emotional intelligence is highlighted by the fact that deficiencies in any of these branches can have far-reaching consequences for others.

When considered in the workplace context, the significance of these four branches becomes increasingly apparent. Regarding professional settings, emotional intelligence is a significant factor in leadership, teamwork effectiveness, and overall company success. Leaders with a high level of self-awareness can identify their strengths and flaws, enabling them to make decisions based on accurate information and help them inspire confidence in their colleagues. By allowing the leaders to maintain their composure in the face of pressure, effective self-regulation contributes to creating a positive working environment. Both social awareness and relationship management abilities are essential for efficient communication, collaboration, and conflict resolution. Social awareness enables leaders to comprehend the requirements and worries of their team members, while relationship management skills facilitate it.

Additionally, emotional intelligence is increasingly regarded as crucial in personnel selection and advancement procedures. Not only do employers reward individuals who possess technical talents, but they also value those who demonstrate emotional intelligence in their relationships with others. A key component of professional success is the capacity to collaborate effectively with people, manage stress effectively, and handle difficult situations successfully. Individuals who possess a high level of emotional intelligence make a significant contribution to a constructive culture in the workplace, which improves collaboration, employee satisfaction, and the firm's overall performance.

Within educational institutions, the four subfields of emotional intelligence play a crucial part in the growth and development of students. Students with a high level of self-awareness are better able to handle the problems they have in their academic lives. They can recognize their preferred methods of learning and address areas that present opportunities for progress. Self-regulation skills are essential for effectively managing stress, maintaining focus, and persevering through the hurdles of academic work. Through the development of social awareness, children can negotiate social dynamics, cultivate healthy connections with their classmates and teachers, and contribute to an atmosphere conducive to learning. Regarding group activities and initiatives that require collaboration, managing relationships, communicating effectively, and resolving conflicts are necessary.

It is important to note that the influence of emotional intelligence extends beyond the human and organizational levels and into the societal and global dimensions. Individuals with a high level of emotional intelligence can traverse the various cultural norms that exist in an interconnected world, communicate well with people from different backgrounds, and contribute to the construction of bridges of understanding. Socially and emotionally intelligent leaders are more suited to manage complex societal concerns and support methods of problem-solving that are inclusive and empathic. The development of emotional intelligence on a more widespread scale contributes to the creation of a global community that is more empathetic and interconnected.

It is vital to acknowledge that emotional intelligence is a dynamic and ever-evolving skill set, even though the four branches of emotional intelligence give a comprehensive framework for understanding human behavior. It is possible to cultivate and improve it through self-reflection, practice, and conscious attempts to deepen each dimension. Individuals can access various interventions, such as mindfulness practices, emotional intelligence training programs, and therapy techniques, which provide them with the tools necessary to improve their emotional intelligence.

In conclusion, the four subfields of emotional intelligence, which are self-awareness, self-regulation, social awareness, and relationship management, combine to produce a sophisticated and all-encompassing framework for comprehending and navigating the complexity associated with human emotions. The interconnectedness of these dimensions allows them to exert a dynamic influence on one another. A growing emphasis is on cultivating and utilizing these skills to achieve personal and community well-being. This is because individuals, companies, and societies are becoming more aware of the significant impact that emotional intelligence has. In the complex terrain of human feelings, the continual investigation of emotional intelligence paves the way for opportunities for personal development, resiliency, and constructive transformation.

Assessing and Developing Emotional Intelligence

Recognizing emotional intelligence as a vital component of personal and professional success has increased interest in assessing and developing this critical skill set. When compared to traditional methods of evaluating intelligence, which emphasizes cognitive capabilities, emotional intelligence places more emphasis on the ability to comprehend and control one's own emotions as well as the feelings of others; within the scope of this section, we will investigate the techniques that are utilized to evaluate emotional intelligence, the significance of such evaluations in both personal and professional settings, as well as the approaches that can be used to cultivate and improve emotional intelligence.

To evaluate an individual's emotional intelligence, one must assess their proficiency level in the essential components of this comprehensive skill set. Numerous instruments and approaches have been developed to evaluate emotional intelligence, each of which places an emphasis on a particular facet of this construct. The Emotional Intelligence Appraisal, which Travis Bradberry and Jean Greaves developed, is an extensively utilized tool. This instrument evaluates an individual's self-awareness, self-regulation, social awareness, and relationship management skills. Another well-known instrument is the Mayer-Salovey-Caruso Emotional Intelligence Test (MSCEIT), designed to assess an individual's emotional intelligence by utilizing the ability model established by the individuals who developed the test by Peter Salovey and John D. Mayer.

Typically, these evaluations consist of self-report questionnaires, in which individuals evaluate their emotional capabilities, and performance-based tests, in which individuals are required to solve emotional problems or respond to emotionally charged scenarios. Although self-report tests offer insights into individuals' beliefs of their passionate talents, performance-based assessments objectively evaluate actual emotional intelligence skills. Self-report measures are the most common type of assessment. A thorough picture of an individual's dynamic intelligence profile can be obtained by combining the two different types of evaluations.

One of the most important reasons to evaluate emotional intelligence is its implications for personal growth, effective leadership, and general well-being. Those with high emotional intelligence are better able to traverse the intricacies of interpersonal interactions, effectively manage stress, and make judgments that are suitable for their circumstances. Individuals are guided on a path of self-discovery and development through assessments, which offer them vital insights about their strengths and areas where they could improve. In addition, organizations are becoming more aware of the significance of emotional intelligence in leadership roles, and evaluations are becoming increasingly valuable tools for finding and cultivating emotionally intelligent leaders.

Because businesses are placing a greater emphasis on cultivating a constructive and cooperative corporate culture, evaluating emotional intelligence is becoming increasingly prevalent in the workplace. Individuals who possess a high level of emotional intelligence can inspire and encourage their teams, cultivate good communication, and handle issues via diplomacy. Increased employee happiness, less employee turnover, and enhanced organizational performance are all clear indicators of the influence that emotionally intelligent leadership has. It is common practice for organizations to incorporate emotional intelligence evaluations into the hiring and promotion procedures to discover individuals who have the potential to make a positive contribution to the atmosphere of the workplace.

Emotional intelligence is a dynamic and ongoing process that requires self-awareness, intentional practice, and a commitment to personal progress. This process is characterized by the involvement of all three of these components. The strategies for building emotional intelligence address many aspects of the skill set. These include self-awareness, self-regulation, social awareness, and relationship management.

The cultivation of mindfulness and reflection are two practices necessary for enhancing self-awareness, which is the primary branch of emotional intelligence. Individuals can improve their understanding of their feelings, triggers, and patterns of behavior by engaging in practices such as journaling, meditation, or exercises that include self-reflection by engaging in these activities. When people have a greater awareness of themselves, they can better identify the influence of their feelings on their decision-making and their relationships with others. This results in a more intentional and genuine approach to life.

Mindfulness practices and approaches for emotion regulation are two methods that can be utilized to cultivate self-regulation, which is the capacity to manage and control one's feelings. Mindfulness is a practice that teaches people to examine their thoughts and feelings without passing judgment on them. This creates an environment in which individuals can respond intentionally rather than reacting on impulse. Individuals can negotiate stressful situations with coolness and resilience by employing deep breathing, visualization, and cognitive restructuring techniques.

It is possible to develop social awareness, which is the ability to comprehend other people's feelings, by engaging in activities that involve active listening and the development of empathy. Learning to tune into non- verbal cues, acknowledging the viewpoints of others, and appreciating the variety of emotional experiences are all necessary steps in developing social awareness. Engaging in meaningful conversations, attempting to comprehend various points of view, and engaging in empathy training are all activities that help the development of this essential aspect of emotional intelligence.

The ability to effectively navigate social relationships is referred to as relationship management. Relationship management is a talent that may be improved by making conscious efforts to improve communication and conflict resolution skills. Individuals can improve their relationship management abilities by actively seeking feedback, practicing assertive communication, and establishing techniques for conflict resolution. The development of effective relationships requires the promotion of collaboration, the establishment of trust, and the modification of communication styles to accommodate a variety of situations and persons.

In the context of education, the cultivation of emotional intelligence is becoming more acknowledged as an essential component of the success and well-being of students. Students are taught skills such as self-awareness, self-regulation, and interpersonal communication through social-emotional learning (SEL) programs implemented at educational institutions. The goal of these programs is to improve students' emotional intelligence. Students are equipped with the practical tools necessary to negotiate the emotional problems they face in academic and social situations through the implementation of SEL programs, promoting resilience and general mental well-being.

Organizations can create training programs and seminars centered on developing emotional intelligence in places of professional exposure. To strengthen emotional intelligence skills, these programs may include activities such as role-playing situations, interactive exercises, and applications that are relevant to the actual world. To establish a culture that appreciates and prioritizes the development of emotionally intelligent skills, leaders can serve as models of emotionally intelligent behavior. Mentorship programs and coaching are two more ways individuals can receive individualized direction and support to improve their emotional intelligence.

Socialtribute to tcan broad development of emotional intelligence and the efforts of individuals and organizations, respectively. The incorporation of dynamic intelligence education into the curriculum of schools, the promotion of awareness campaigns, and the provision of resources for individuals to improve their emotional intelligence can all contribute to the development of a society that is more empathic and emotionally intelligent. The formation of emotionally intelligent communities is facilitated by recognizing emotional intelligence as a critical ability in various sectors, including education, healthcare, and leadership.

enhancing one's emotional intelligence are vital to personal and professional development. Individuals and organizations can get valuable insights into their emotional strengths and areas where they could grow through assessments, guiding intentional actions toward improving emotional intelligence. Tactics for development include self-awareness, self-regulation, social awareness, and relationship management. These tactics are designed to address the complex character of emotional intelligence. The continual commitment to evaluating and developing emotional intelligence becomes a catalyst for positive personal, organizational, and social transformation as society progressively acknowledges the relevance of emotional intelligence in navigating the intricacies of human interactions.

CHAPTER III

Identifying and Recognizing Emotions

Understanding Different Emotions

Emotions, the intricate tapestry of human experience, shape how we perceive and respond to the world around us. Emotions are the vivid colors that create the picture of our lives, ranging from the thrill of excitement to the depths of grief. Comprehending these varied emotional experiences is essential to emotional intelligence and a fundamental element of human connection. We shall examine the wide range of emotions in this section, including their causes, the intricacy of their expressions, and their enormous influence on our attitudes, actions, and interpersonal interactions.

Emotions are complex physiological and psychological reactions to internal and external events. They cover many emotions, from simple, primordial responses to intricate, subtle sensations. Primary emotions are fundamental to our emotional experiences; they are inborn, universal reactions that cut across social and cultural divides. These emotions serve vital adaptive roles in human survival, including happiness, sadness, fear, rage, surprise, and disgust. Our biology is programmed with primary emotions, which enable us to react quickly and intuitively to a wide range of circumstances and warn us of impending dangers, rewards, or environmental changes.

In addition to primary emotions, people also feel a wide range of secondary emotions that result from the interaction between fundamental emotions and cognitive functions. Frequently, secondary emotions are more intricate, combining to produce subtle emotional states. Awe or wonder, for instance, might arise when surprise and joy blend. Fear and grief together have the potential to cause uneasiness or trepidation. These auxiliary feelings, which represent the complexity of our emotional and cognitive landscapes, add to the richness of our emotional experiences.

Cultural and social factors greatly influence emotional expression and understanding. Although the primary emotions are known to everyone, how they are interpreted and expressed might vary depending on the cultural setting. People perceive emotions differently due to individual variances, societal expectations, and cultural conventions. For example, although some cultures respect emotional restraint and stoicism, others may encourage the unrestricted expression of emotions. Since misinterpretations can result in misunderstandings and disputes, it is essential to comprehend the cultural nuances of feelings to have good communication and build interpersonal connections.

The study of emotions is a central theme in many psychological theories and methods. Through his seminal research on facial expressions, psychologist Paul Ekman discovered a set of common facial expressions that correlate to primary emotions. The survey of Ekman, whose work is popularly referred to as the Facial Action Coding System (FACS), established the foundation for our knowledge of nonverbal signs in emotional communication. Similarly, Robert Plutchik's Wheel of Emotions offers a thorough model that classifies feelings into core and secondary groups and shows the intricate connections between various emotional states. These theoretical frameworks give essential insights into the dynamics and structure of emotions, laying the groundwork for future investigations and real-world applications in disciplines including communication studies, psychology, and sociology.

Psychology also delves into emotional intelligence, stressing how crucial it is to identify, comprehend, and control emotions to succeed both individually and in social situations. Several components of emotional intelligence were identified by psychologist Daniel Goleman, who played a significant role in popularizing the term. These components include self-awareness, self-regulation, social awareness, and relationship management. These elements emphasize the versatility of emotional intelligence and the capacity to manage emotions in various situations successfully.

Recognizing and comprehending one's emotions is a necessary part of self-awareness, a facet of emotional intelligence. Emotional intelligence is built on this reflective capacity, which enables people to recognize their emotional states, understand the causes of their emotions, and remember how their emotions may affect their ideas and actions. Being self-aware is a lifelong practice of introspection that gives people knowledge about their emotional assets, weaknesses, and potential growth areas.

Effective management and control of one's emotions is called self-regulation, another essential element of emotional intelligence. This dimension entails overcoming difficult circumstances without letting bad feelings get the better of you. Strong self-regulation abilities enable people to remain composed, make wise choices, and adjust to changing situations—the ability to control one's impulses and postpone satisfaction benefits long-term goal achievement and general mental health.

Emotional intelligence is centered on social awareness, which transcends personal reflection. This dimension deals with the capacity to recognize and comprehend other people's feelings. People with high social awareness can detect nonverbal clues, empathize with others, and understand the emotional dynamics of a situation. This ability is essential for managing connections with others, encouraging clear communication, and developing rapport. Socially conscious people can decipher subtle social signs and modify their conduct to fit the emotional requirements of various contexts and people.

The last facet of emotional intelligence, relationship management, includes a variety of skills for productive social interactions. Building and sustaining healthy relationships requires an awareness of emotions, which is the focus of this dimension. People with good relationship management abilities can handle the intricacies of group dynamics, communicate assertively, and settle disputes graciously. This area of emotional intelligence is significant for those in leadership positions since these individuals need to inspire and motivate others, form cooperative networks, and foster a favorable work atmosphere.

How people move through and react to the emotional terrain of interpersonal relationships demonstrates the link between emotional intelligence and knowing various emotions. The general success and pleasure in both personal and professional contexts is influenced by the capacity to identify and comprehend one's emotions, control emotional reactions, perceive the feelings of others, and effectively manage relationships.

One of the most important aspects of knowing different emotions is the effect that emotions have on cognition and decision-making. Affective neuroscience research has uncovered the complex interplay between emotions and cognitive functions. Emotions can affect perception and interpretation of information, attention, memory, and judgment. For instance, being in a good mood might help you be more creative and adept at solving problems, but worry or anxiety can make it harder to concentrate and make decisions. Comprehending these intricacies is imperative to make knowledgeable decisions, cultivate psychological equilibrium, and advance proficient correspondence.

Emotions also significantly impact how identity is shaped and how one feels about themselves. Developing a cohesive and genuine self-concept is facilitated by investigating and comprehending one's emotional terrain. Accepting a broad spectrum of emotions, even uncomfortable or difficult, promotes resilience and self-acceptance. People adept at managing and integrating various emotions can better handle life's obstacles, form enduring bonds with others, and seek meaning and fulfillment.

Understanding various emotions is essential for efficient communication and empathy in interpersonal relationships. A sophisticated comprehension of diverse emotions, which is the ability to comprehend and experience another person's experiences, is necessary for empathy. People with empathy can tune into other people's emotional experiences and provide connection, affirmation, and support. Relationship quality is improved by identifying and reacting to various emotions, which promotes closeness, trust, and understanding.

To effectively handle conflicts and obstacles, one of the most important aspects of interpersonal dynamics is conflict resolution, which calls for an awareness of emotions. People who can detect, express, and perceive the feelings of others are better able to have productive conversations and come up with solutions that benefit both parties. Understanding the range of emotions helps people communicate effectively, which lowers the possibility of miscommunication and fosters happy relationships.

The way that certain emotions are understood and expressed is greatly influenced by the cultural background. Cultural norms, values, and societal expectations shape how emotions are understood and defined. For example, cultural acceptance of emotional expressiveness might differ; some cultures value emotional restraint, while others promote candid emotional expression. Comprehending these cultural subtleties is crucial for cross-cultural.

-intercultural dialogue and fostering relationships with people from different backgrounds. Misreading emotional cues can cause miscommunication and misunderstandings, emphasizing how crucial cultural awareness is when negotiating the emotional terrain.

The study of emotions has applications in philosophy, literature, and the arts in addition to psychology. As a mirror of the human condition, literature delves into the depths of various emotions. It provides insights into the intricacies of interpersonal interactions and the mind's inner workings. Mixed emotions are embodied by characters in plays, novels, and poetry, giving readers a mirror to look at and relate to the universal features of the human condition while also reflecting on their own emotional experiences.

Creative expressions effectively express and evoke feelings, whether they come from dance, music, or visual arts. Artists employ color, form, melody, and movement to elicit distinct emotional reactions from their audience. This results in a shared emotional experience between the artist and the viewer. Through art, people can explore and express their emotions in novel and transforming ways that cut beyond language barriers and establish emotional connections.

Philosophy explores the nature of emotions, raising issues regarding their genesis, importance, and moral ramifications. Philosophers have examined the significance of emotions in human existence throughout history, ranging from existentialist views on the emotional complexity of human freedom and responsibility to Aristotle's consideration of virtue and emotions. The philosophical discussion around emotions advances our knowledge of their conceptual foundations and how they affect human morality and decision-making.

The study of emotions is becoming more prevalent in artificial intelligence (AI) as technology develops. To provide AI systems the ability to perceive and react to human emotions, scientists and engineers are investigating methods to endow them with emotional intelligence. Applications for emotionally intelligent AI may arise in fields like healthcare, education, and customer service, where these systems improve human experiences by recognizing and adjusting to various emotional states.

Conclusively, comprehending diverse emotions is an intricate undertaking, including several fields such as psychology, culture, literature, art, philosophy, and technology. Emotions permeate every aspect of the human experience, impacting how we see ourselves, relate to others, and negotiate the challenges of daily existence. In addition to affording opportunities for efficient communication, personal development, and creating compassionate and supportive communities, the study of emotions offers insightful information on the complexity and diversity of the human emotional landscape. We set out on a path of self-discovery and group understanding as we continue to explore the complexities of emotions, accepting the rainbow of emotions that paint the picture of our shared human experience.

The Importance of Emotional Awareness

The ability to detect, comprehend, and manage feelings is fundamental to emotional intelligence and general well-being. Emotional awareness is the ability to do all of these things. In a society that frequently places a premium on intellectual capabilities and academic accomplishments, the relevance of emotional awareness is sometimes disregarded. On the other hand, having the capacity to recognize and understand one's feelings has far-reaching ramifications for several aspects of one's life, including personal development, mental health, and the quality of interpersonal relationships. In this section, we will investigate the tremendous significance of emotional awareness by analyzing its function in the process of self-discovery, resiliency, decision-making, and the development of social connections that are empathic and harmonious.

Emotional awareness can be broken down into its most fundamental components, including being attuned to one's own emotional states and aware of the wide variety of sentiments that various circumstances can generate. In psychology, Peter Salovey and John D. Mayer are credited with popularizing the concept of emotional intelligence, which Daniel Goleman built upon. This self-awareness serves as the cornerstone of emotional intelligence. When developing other aspects of emotional intelligence, such as self-regulation, social awareness, and relationship management, recognizing and comprehending one's feelings is the foundation for developing these aspects.

It is not enough to be aware of when one is pleased, sad, or furious; self-awareness of emotions requires more than that. A thorough understanding of the underlying causes and inciting factors for these feelings is needed to accomplish this. For instance, a deeper level of emotional awareness can be achieved by acknowledging that a surge of delight is a reaction to personal accomplishments or that a sense of irritation may result from expectations that have not been completely fulfilled. Through this reflective skill, individuals can investigate the complexities of their emotional environment, ultimately resulting in a more profound understanding of each individual.

One of the most essential advantages of emotional awareness is its function in developing resilience. Life is full of obstacles, failures, and ambiguities, all of which have the potential to elicit a wide range of feelings, ranging from dissatisfaction and frustration to worry and anxiety. When confronted with such circumstances, persons who possess a heightened emotional awareness are better able to handle these feelings confidently. They can recognize and process their feelings, which allows them to build coping skills that encourage resilience and adaptive reactions to adversity. This will enable them to avoid becoming overwhelmed or giving in to unpleasant sentiments.

When it comes to making decisions, emotional awareness acts as a compass, impacting the choices individuals make in various facets of their lives. Individuals who are emotionally aware can take into consideration not only the cognitive parts of a decision but also the emotional ramifications of that decision when confronted with difficult choices. One's ideals, objectives, and emotional well-being are all considered during this integrated decision-making process, which ultimately leads to conclusions that make sense. Evaluating the emotional consequences of decisions is a positive factor that contributes to a more genuine and purposeful path through life.

Additionally, emotional awareness is an essential component in the process of cultivating mental health and enlarging well-being. When it comes to sustaining a mental state that is both balanced and resilient, the identification and acceptance of emotions are essential things to do. Repressing or disregarding one's feelings can result in internal conflicts and stress and, in the long term, contribute to difficulties with one's mental health. On the other hand, individuals who embrace emotional awareness are more equipped to manage stress, navigate through problems, and seek appropriate support when required. When laying the groundwork for general well-being, this preventative approach to mental health is essential.

The ability to communicate effectively, essential to maintaining successful relationships, strongly depends on emotional awareness. When individuals can comprehend and articulate their feelings clearly and concisely, it improves their capacity to communicate naturally and establish a more profound connection with other people. Also, those with emotional awareness can identify and react appropriately to the feelings of those in their immediate vicinity. The cultivation of compassionate communication, the reduction of misconceptions, and the contribution to the development of social settings that are helpful and nurturing are all outcomes of this empathic understanding.

It is essential to be emotionally aware when it comes to the context of interpersonal relationships, as this is the most effective way to resolve problems and establish deep connections. Disagreements frequently emerge due to divergent points of view, unfulfilled emotional needs, or inadequate communication. People with a high emotional awareness can manage these issues with empathy and understanding, thereby addressing the emotional undercurrents that may be the source of discord. Individuals can form deeper connections with one another and deepen the bonds of trust in their relationships if they make an effort to truly express their emotions and listen to others with an open mind.

It is the responsibility of parents and teachers to play a crucial part in the development of emotional awareness in children and adolescents. For young people to successfully traverse the complexities of their feelings, they must receive direction and assistance to comprehend and articulate their emotions. Through incorporating emotional awareness education into standard school curricula and parental strategies, children are equipped with the tools necessary to traverse the dynamic landscapes they encounter correctly. The development of emotionally resilient persons who are better prepared for the challenges of adulthood is facilitated by this early investment in emotional intelligence, leading to the development of emotionally resilient individuals.

The cultivation of emotional awareness can be accomplished through practical techniques such as meditation and self-reflection, which are mindful practices. Individuals are encouraged to notice their thoughts and feelings without passing judgment through these techniques, which helps cultivate a non-reactive and receptive attitude toward their internal experiences.

Individuals can develop a heightened level of awareness via mindfulness, which enables them to recognize emotions as they occur, comprehend the impact they have, and respond with intentionality. Individuals can negotiate stressors, improve their self-regulating ability, and create a more present and focused way of living as mindfulness becomes an intrinsic part of daily life.

Emotional regulation, the capacity to control and modify one's emotional responses, is also closely connected to emotional conscious awareness. People who are emotionally aware can recognize when their feelings are becoming more intense and implement tactics that will allow them to control those feelings effectively. This type of self-regulation not only contributes to mental well-being but also improves interpersonal relationships by minimizing the escalation of conflicts and generating a more constructive emotional climate.

In the area of professional life, emotional awareness is becoming more and more recognized as an essential component of good leadership. Leaders who can navigate the dynamic landscapes of their teams and have a good understanding of their own emotions are better suited to inspire, motivate, and lead with empathy. The capacity to identify and respond to the feelings of team members helps to cultivate a positive atmosphere at work, increases the level of satisfaction experienced by employees, and adds to the organization's overall success. Organizations that prioritize emotional intelligence in their leadership development initiatives frequently observe benefits in teamwork, communication, and employee engagement throughout the organization.

The growth of emotional awareness is an ongoing process that requires regular self-reflection and conscious efforts to comprehend and manage one's feelings. Individuals are provided with a safe environment in which they can investigate and work through their feelings through the use of therapeutic procedures such as psychotherapy and counseling.

Techniques and procedures designed to improve emotional awareness are frequently incorporated into these therapies. As a result, individuals are given the ability to cultivate healthy connections with themselves and with others.

Regarding the value of emotional awareness, it is impossible to overstate its significance. It is a fundamental component of emotional intelligence, and it plays a role in developing personal growth, resilience, the ability to make sound decisions, and the establishment of harmonious relationships. Individuals can harness the potential for self-discovery and negotiate life's obstacles with greater authenticity and purpose when they accept the complexity of their emotional landscapes and embrace them. In addition to being a voyage of self-reflection, the continuing cultivation of emotional awareness is also a transformative process that expands the tapestry of human experience and nurtures a more empathic and interdependent world.

Practical Exercises for Recognizing Emotions

Fundamental competencies in emotional intelligence include the ability to identify and comprehend emotions. Emotional intelligence—the capacity to recognize and understand one's emotions and those of others—plays a critical role in self-control, meaningful relationship formation, and effective communication. Though emotional awareness is essential, hands-on activities provide concrete ways for people to actively interact with and improve their emotional awareness. This section will examine a range of valuable activities intended to develop the ability to identify emotions in people, giving them essential tools for better interpersonal relationships and personal development.

Keeping an emotion journal is one of the basic exercises for identifying emotions. This activity encourages people to consider and record their emotional experiences routinely. People can register in their journals the particular feelings they are experiencing, the circumstances that lead to these emotions, and any related ideas or bodily experiences. Through this process, people can become more self-aware and recognize patterns and trends in their emotional reactions. An emotion journal is helpful for introspection because it helps people gain a deeper awareness of their dynamic landscape and acts as a point of reference for monitoring personal development.

Recognizing emotions through mindfulness meditation is another effective practice. Being mindful entails focusing one's attention on the ideas and feelings that are happening right now without passing judgment. During a mindfulness meditation session, people might concentrate on the feelings connected to various emotions. A person's emotional awareness can be increased by observing emotions objectively and without bias. Frequent mindfulness practice improves the relationship between the mind and body, making it possible for people to respond more clearly and purposefully to even the most minor changes in their emotional states.

The "Body Scan" exercise is a mindfulness practice that improves emotional recognition by encouraging a systematic awareness of physical sensations. During this practice, people mentally scan their body, focusing on tense, sore, or relaxed regions. Physical manifestations of emotions are common, and the body scan helps establish a link between these physical experiences and underlying emotional states. People can better comprehend their moving experiences and apply this information to self-regulation by learning to recognize the biological indicators of emotions.

Emotion wheels and charts are examples of visual aids that can be useful for identifying and classifying emotions. Usually, these gadgets show a variety of emotions and their matching facial expressions. People can use these images to recognize and categorize their feelings when faced with a specific emotion. Through this practice, people's emotional language and ability to express their feelings are improved. Furthermore, in educational or group contexts, visual aids can help generate conversations about emotions and a shared understanding of the range of emotional experiences that people can have.

Developing a deeper understanding of emotions can also be achieved through reflective writing assignments. People can understand their feelings' underlying reasons and implications by responding to stimuli that foster emotional exploration. Reflective writing makes a more complex comprehension of the dynamic landscape possible, which offers an organized forum for emotional expression. Through journaling, sections, or creative writing, this practice helps people become more self-aware and emotionally intelligent by pushing them to explore the depths of their feelings.

Recognizing and expressing emotions is made fun and participatory with the "Emotion Charades" activity. In this game, players take turns assuming various emotional states while remaining silent, and other players attempt to identify the state each player is thinking. Through this practice, you can improve your nonverbal communication skills and become more aware of the gestures, body language, and facial expressions that convey different emotions. People strengthen their capacity to identify and understand emotions by actively experiencing and monitoring emotions in this lighthearted setting.

Examining art to identify feelings offers a creative way to express oneself. Through the medium of drawing, painting, or sculpture, people can externalize their inner experiences. Using art as a therapeutic medium, people can explore and reflect on complicated feelings that are difficult to express verbally. Moreover, art can be a helpful communication tool in therapeutic contexts, giving people a nonverbal way to express their emotional experiences.

The "Three-Word Check-In" is a brief yet effective activity that helps group members identify emotions. Each person takes a turn using just three words to describe their feelings. This practice encourages people to condense their feelings into a concise and targeted expression, promoting emotional communication accuracy and clarity. The three-word restriction forces participants to identify and communicate the most essential parts of their emotional experience, fostering effective group communication and self-awareness.

Integrating literature and storytelling into the study of emotions provides a narrative framework for identifying and comprehending a range of emotional experiences. People can relate to various viewpoints and feelings by reading literature that explores characters' emotional lives. Talking in groups about the motivations and emotions of the characters might help participants reflect on their own lives and improve their capacity to identify and relate to a wide range of emotional states.

Using guided visualization, the "Emotion-Focused Imagery" exercise helps participants explore and identify emotions in a more sensory-rich way. Participants visualize a particular situation or memory connected to a certain feeling with their eyes closed. People might develop a deeper emotional connection with the visualization by fully submerging themselves in it. By improving the vividness and clarity of emotional memories, this activity helps people comprehend the related feelings more complexly.

Developing empathy via perspective-taking activities is an effective method of identifying other people's feelings. This is purposefully putting yourself in another person's shoes and considering their feelings, ideas, and experiences. As people become more aware of the range of emotional experiences, perspective-taking promotes social awareness. Exercises that teach people to identify and value the feelings of others help them develop empathy, a crucial aspect of emotional intelligence.

Technological tools, including internet resources or applications for identifying emotions, can help further with emotion recognition. Using face recognition technology, these instruments frequently evaluate and recognize emotions from facial expressions. Although these applications cannot replace self-awareness exercises, they can be helpful as additional resources for people looking for immediate feedback on how they are expressing their emotions. Technology-driven activities can benefit those who would instead handle emotional recognition in a systematic, data-driven manner.

A quick and easy way to improve emotional awareness is to use the "Daily Emotional Check-In" habit. People pause every day at the end of the day to think back on the feelings they had during the day. Consistent self-awareness is fostered by this everyday exercise, which also helps people recognize emotional patterns or triggers over time. Establishing the emotional check-in as a regular practice allows people to form reflective and mindfulness habits, which support the continuous emotional identification and comprehension process.

Individuals can identify and communicate their feelings in a helpful setting by participating in group therapy or support groups. People might discover similarities and contrasts in how emotions are expressed and processed in group settings because they provide a variety of viewpoints and emotional experiences. In a group setting, the collective examination of feelings promotes understanding and a sense of belonging.

In summary, hands-on tasks that include identifying emotions greatly aid in building emotional intelligence and improving interpersonal skills. Through practical techniques for actively engaging with emotions, these activities help people develop self-awareness, empathy, and effective communication. Through creative expression, writing, mindfulness exercises, or group activities, these beneficial activities help cultivate a more nuanced awareness of the complex world of emotions. By incorporating these activities into everyday routines and interpersonal interactions, people can develop an elevated emotional awareness, leading to personal development and strengthening social bonds.

CHAPTER IV

Emotional Regulation Techniques

Managing Negative Emotions

A necessary component of the human experience is negativity. Negative emotions can surface in reaction to various obstacles and pressures, from sadness and worry to irritation and wrath. A key component of emotional intelligence is effectively managing these emotions, which promotes general wellbeing and success in interpersonal relationships. In this section, we will discuss the importance of controlling negative emotions, the effects of unresolved negativity on mental health, and doable tactics for developing emotional resilience.

Even though they are frequently categorized as unpleasant or unwelcome, negative emotions are necessary for human existence. Even though they can not be enjoyable, these feelings provide essential insights into a person's internal condition and external surroundings. Anger, for instance, may indicate a perceived injustice or boundary breach, which would lead people to confront and correct the problem. Like other emotions, sorrow can be a sign of a loss or an unfulfilled need, emphasizing the significance of processing and comprehending these feelings instead of repressing or avoiding them.

Effective emotion regulation starts with accepting and recognizing negative feelings. Denying or suppressing these feelings can have long-term detrimental effects on mental health, in addition to increasing stress and internal tensions. Conversely, recognizing and comprehending negative feelings allow people to deal with underlying problems, create coping mechanisms, and build emotional resilience.

Negative emotions that are not controlled can have a severe effect on mental health. When untreated, enduring emotions of melancholy, rage, or fear can hasten the onset of mental health conditions, including depression or anxiety disorders. Chronic stress brought on by an incapacity to control unpleasant emotions has been connected to physical health concerns like weakened immune systems and cardiovascular difficulties. Understanding the possible repercussions of unchecked negativity emphasizes how critical it is to develop healthy coping mechanisms for unpleasant feelings.

A crucial element in handling negative feelings is growing self-awareness. Being self-aware entails acknowledging and comprehending one's feelings without passing judgment. People with a high level of self-awareness can recognize negative emotions when they occur, pinpoint the exact causes, and understand the emotional reaction patterns. The capacity for introspection is essential for proficient emotional regulation because it enables people to step in and initiate coping mechanisms before unfavorable feelings intensify.

Meditation and mindful breathing are two effective mindfulness techniques for handling unpleasant emotions. Being mindful entails focusing one's attention on the ideas and feelings that are happening right now without passing judgment. People who practice mindfulness can perceive negative feelings without becoming caught up in them. Instead of reacting impulsively to unpleasant emotions, people can respond to them intentionally when they have this non-reactive awareness. Frequent mindfulness practice has been linked to better emotional regulation, lower stress levels, and overall well-being.

Cognitive-behavioral techniques, which target the underlying cognitive processes that lead to emotional distress, provide practical methods for handling negative emotions. The goal of cognitive-behavioral therapy (CBT), a therapeutic approach, is to recognize and confront harmful thought patterns and replace them with more realistic and adaptive beliefs. People can improve their coping strategies and emotional reactions by reorganizing their faulty cognitive processes. With an emphasis on the connections between ideas, feelings, and behaviors, cognitive behavioral therapy (CBT) has shown promise in the treatment of several mental health issues.

Expressive writing is a therapeutic method that helps

people express and write about unpleasant feelings. This procedure involves verbalizing feelings to allow them to externalize and process them. Expressive writing encourages introspection and an awareness of one's emotions by exploring unpleasant feelings' root causes and effects. Pent-up feelings can be released, and a sense of emotional relief can be gained via the cathartic writing process.

Having social support is essential for controlling bad

feelings. Speaking with dependable family members, friends, or mental health specialists about one's emotions can offer support, understanding, and other viewpoints. Sharing feelings makes people feel more connected to one another and less isolated, which is a common side effect of negative emotions. Social support networks give people a place to get direction, inspiration, and helpful counsel for overcoming obstacles.

Exercise and physical activity have been connected to

better mental and emotional health. Frequent physical activity lowers stress hormone levels and releases endorphins, the body's natural mood enhancers. Physical activity, whether in strength training, cardiovascular workouts, or yoga, offers a comprehensive strategy for handling negative emotions by fostering mental and physical health. Exercise's repetitive and rhythmic qualities can reduce stress and maintain emotional equilibrium by relaxing the mind.

Reframing negative emotions and developing a positive perspective can be achieved through the transformative method of practicing gratitude. Being grateful is making a conscious effort to notice and value the good things in one's life. This can be achieved by engaging in routines like maintaining a daily thankfulness diary, where people list their blessings. One way to foster optimism and lessen the effects of negative emotions is to refocus attention from what is lacking or harmful to what is affirming and positive.

Developing time management and prioritization skills is essential in avoiding the build-up of stressors that fuel negative emotions. Abundant duties or responsibilities can make one feel overburdened, increasing tension and worry. People can lower their risk of chronic stress and the bad feelings that come with it by prioritizing their responsibilities, managing their time well, and setting realistic goals. Maintaining mental health requires balancing work, play, and self-care.

One of the most important aspects of handling negative emotions in interpersonal relationships is setting healthy limits. Setting up courteous and unambiguous boundaries aids people in safeguarding their emotional health and preserving positive relationships with others. Emotional resilience is influenced by knowing when to back down from difficult situations, expressing demands, and setting personal boundaries. By defining and upholding boundaries, one can avoid the emotional costs associated with overextending oneself and foster a sense of autonomy and self-care.

People can channel and release unpleasant emotions through artistic expression, whether it is through music, visual arts, or other creative avenues. People can externalize their interior experiences and communicate emotions that may be difficult to express through art.

Art as a therapeutic tool can help people explore the nuances of their emotional terrain and let go of pent-up feelings. Taking part in the creative process can also make you feel happy and accomplished, which helps lessen the effects of unpleasant emotions.

A sound and frequently underappreciated strategy for controlling destructive emotions is humor. Endorphins are released when we laugh, which improves our mood and lowers stress levels. Whether via jokes, comedy, or lighthearted activities, incorporating humor into daily life can help to promote a more positive emotional state and act as a diversion from negative feelings. Even in dire circumstances, finding humor can provide a new viewpoint and increase one's ability to bounce back from setbacks.

Self-compassion is the act of being compassionate and understanding to oneself, especially when facing difficulties or failing. Those who practice self-compassion give themselves the same support and encouragement they would provide to a friend going through a similar situation, as opposed to harsh judgment or self-criticism. Acknowledging flaws, embracing vulnerability, and realizing that it doesn't feel good are standard parts of human development and are all necessary components of self-compassion.There is no one-size-fits-all approach to handling negative emotions, and people may discover that a mix of

Strategies that work best for them. People can customize their coping mechanisms to suit their requirements and inclinations by trying various approaches and monitoring how they affect their emotional health. Additionally, getting expert advice from mental health specialists like therapists or counselors can offer people individualized techniques and support for handling difficult emotions.

Controlling negative emotions is a dynamic, continuous process that calls for self-awareness, grit, and deliberate effort. People can develop emotional resilience and stop mismanaged negativity's long-term effects on mental health by recognizing, comprehending, and actively addressing unpleasant emotions. Integrating mindfulness practices, cognitive-behavioral methods, social support, and other pragmatic methodologies enables individuals to effectively navigate the intricacies of their emotional landscapes, leading to a more harmonious and satisfying existence.

Cultivating Positive Emotions

Joy, thankfulness, love, contentment, and other positive feelings are essential in determining one's overall quality of life and well-being. In addition to bringing about instant euphoria, nurturing these happy feelings also benefits one's long-term physical and mental wellbeing. This post will discuss the importance of feeling good, how positivity affects all facets of life and doable tactics for creating a happier and more contented emotional environment.

Good feelings are essential to the more significant idea of emotional wellbeing and are frequently linked to greater happiness and life satisfaction. Resilience in the face of adversity and a sense of purpose and fulfillment are enhanced by positive emotional experiences. Positive emotions provide a unique set of advantages beyond fleeting happiness, impacting social relationships, cognitive performance, and physical health and serving vital roles in negative emotions.

Research in positive psychology has emphasized the significance of a positive emotional ratio—the equilibrium between positive and negative emotions—in predicting general wellbeing. People who often experience a larger ratio of good to negative emotions are more likely to report feeling satisfied with their lives, being in better physical health, and living longer. Developing a pleasant emotional state that can mitigate the effects of life's challenges is the goal of cultivating happy emotions, not stifling negative ones.

According to psychologist Barbara Fredrickson's broaden-and-build hypothesis, happy feelings help people see the world more broadly and develop enduring personal resources. Positive emotions allow people to consider and do more options than negative emotions because they provide a more comprehensive range of options. Consequently, this broadened perspective encourages the development of individual assets like adaptability, interpersonal relationships, and coping mechanisms. The broaden-and-build idea emphasizes how profoundly good feelings can improve well-being and personal development.

One of the most studied pleasant emotions is gratitude, which has been repeatedly connected to several psychological and physiological advantages. To cultivate thankfulness, one must intentionally recognize and value the good things in one's life. This can be achieved by engaging in practices such as maintaining a gratitude notebook, in which people routinely list their blessings. Experiencing gratitude not only amplifies happy emotions but also has a role in bettering mental wellbeing, sleep quality, and interpersonal connections. Gratitude is an action that cultivates plenty and contentment by encouraging a good outlook.

Although mindfulness is frequently linked to controlling unpleasant emotions, it can also be quite effective at fostering good emotions. Being mindful entails focusing one's attention on the ideas and feelings that are happening right now without passing judgment. People can ultimately interact with and relish happy events by practicing mindfulness. People who practice mindful awareness can enjoy the fullness of happy feelings without being sidetracked by regrets from the past or worries about the future. Frequent mindfulness practice generally leads to improved emotional health and an enhanced capacity to find joy in ordinary experiences.

Small or large, deeds of kindness have been demonstrated to increase happiness in both the donor and the recipient. Prosocial activities that promote a sense of fulfillment and connection include volunteering, being kind to others, and assisting others. The release of oxytocin, a hormone linked to positive social interactions and bonding, is triggered by acts of kindness. Kindness has a contagious impact beyond the direct exchange and fosters a more sympathetic and upbeat social atmosphere.

Having supportive social networks is essential for fostering happy feelings. An individual's sense of belonging and emotional health are influenced by establishing and maintaining meaningful relationships with friends, family, and the community. Warmth, empathy, and support are the hallmarks of excellent social connections, which build an optimistic emotional bank that may be accessed through trying times. In addition to offering chances for great experiences and a feeling of purpose, social connections also provide emotional support.

Developing positive emotions requires that one partake in activities that make one happy and give them a sense of success. People who pursue interests, hobbies, or creative endeavors can enter a condition known as flow, characterized by total focus and absorption. Painting, singing, gardening, or other passion-driven activities can foster a pleasant emotional state and a sense of fulfillment. Maintaining emotional wellbeing requires balancing work, play, and enjoyable pursuits.

A happy outlook and emotional resilience are facilitated by positive self-talk and affirmations. People's internal dialogue impacts their emotional state and general wellbeing. Developing constructive and uplifting words to replace self-critical or pessimistic ideas is part of cultivating positive self-talk. Repetition of positive comments about oneself or one's objectives or affirmations can be a potent strategy for building self-esteem and a good self-image. Positive self-talk is a deliberate technique that enhances emotional resilience and fosters optimism.

Exercise has been repeatedly linked to the release of endorphins, which are chemicals that naturally elevate mood. Frequent exercise lowers tension, anxiety, and depressive symptoms, which promotes happy feelings. Physical exercise, whether in strength training, cardiovascular activities, or yoga, offers a comprehensive strategy for developing optimism. A pleasant emotional state is influenced by the sense of success, higher vitality, and enhanced general well-being that comes with physical activity.

Laughter is a powerful technique for creating pleasant feelings and is frequently called the finest medicine. Endorphins are released when we laugh, which improves our mood and lowers stress levels. Whether through comedy, jokes, or lighthearted activities, incorporating humor into daily life can improve mood and lead to a more positive emotional state. Laughing is an excellent technique for generating happy feelings in social contexts since it is a social action that builds connections.

Conscientiously visualizing favorable results and experiences is known as positive visualization. Through visualization techniques like guided imagery or mental rehearsal, people can conjure up good, desirable scenarios in their minds. In addition to encouraging optimism, goal-directed behavior and motivation are also improved by positive visualization. People can cultivate an optimistic outlook and boost their confidence in their capacity to succeed by consistently picturing favorable results.

Nature greatly influences emotional wellbeing, and spending time in natural settings is linked to an increase in happy feelings. Nature can be peaceful and revitalizing, whether taking a stroll in a park, trekking in the mountains, or relaxing in a garden. It has been shown that being in natural environments lowers stress and boosts sensations of energy and vitality. People who cultivate a relationship with nature find solace from the stresses of everyday life and a source of positive emotions.

It is possible to deliberately employ music to foster

pleasant moods because it can trigger many emotions. Whether uplifting or peaceful, listening to music that evokes positive feelings can affect mood and help one feel happier. Singing or playing an instrument are examples of music-making activities that give people a direct and interactive opportunity to experience the emotional benefits of music.

Establishing and pursuing important goals bolsters a

sense of purpose and happy feelings. One finds inspiration and fulfillment in pursuing goals consistent with their values and objectives. The quest of objectives fosters feelings of progress and achievement, which supports happy feelings like pride and contentment. By dividing more ambitious objectives into more manageable milestones, people can feel comfortable and content to the finish.

Combining mindfulness and gratitude practices is the

purposeful practice of mindfulness-based gratitude. This method enables people to show thanks for those moments while immersing themselves in happy events. Gratitude grounded in mindfulness deepens pleasant feelings by encouraging an increased awareness and appreciation of the present moment. This exercise is especially beneficial for building resilience and a positive outlook.Positive emotions are developed in educational curricula through positive education initiatives. These courses concentrate on

In addition to standard academic courses, character

strengths, interpersonal connections, and emotional wellbeing are fostered. Pleasant education emphasizes the value of pleasurable emotions in general well-being and attempts to provide students with the knowledge, abilities, and mindset needed for a successful existence.

Incorporating positive education ideas into learning environments facilitates the development of emotionally robust and positively engaged people.

In summary, developing pleasant emotions is a dynamic and deliberate process that enhances general well-being and happiness. People who deliberately cultivate acts of kindness, mindfulness, gratitude, and positive social connections have a positive emotional reserve they may tap into in trying times. A more positive dynamic landscape can be achieved by pursuing essential goals, embracing positive behaviors in daily life, and participating in joyful activities. When people consciously cultivate pleasant emotions, they increase their enjoyment in the moment and create long-lasting personal resources that support a more robust and fulfilling life.

Breathing Exercises, Mindfulness, and Other Techniques

In the fast-paced and often demanding landscape of modern life, individuals face myriad stressors that can impact their mental and physical wellbeing. Effective stress-reduction strategies become essential amid the chaos. This section examines many strategies as practical tools for encouraging relaxation, lowering stress levels, and improving general mental health. These strategies include breathing exercises, mindfulness, and other approaches.

Conscious breathing is an old practice that has found its way into modern wellness tactics and is considered one of the core ways of managing stress. Deep breathing exercises entail slowly inhaling through the nose, letting the diaphragm fully expand, and gradually expelling through pursed lips. Examples of these exercises include diaphragmatic breathing and abdominal breathing. This deliberate attention to breath draws attention to the here and now, encouraging serenity and relaxation. According to science, deep breathing sets off the body's relaxation response, which activates the parasympathetic nerve system and suppresses the fight- or-flight reaction brought on by stress.

With roots in contemplative traditions as old as

Buddhism, mindfulness has been widely acknowledged as an effective stress-reduction method. Being mindful is recognizing thoughts and feelings without getting caught up and focusing on the here and now with no bias. Structured methods for incorporating mindfulness into daily life are provided by mindfulness-based practices like Mindfulness-Based Stress Reduction (MBSR) and Mindfulness-Based Cognitive Therapy (MBCT). By developing an acute awareness of the present, mindfulness enables people to respond to challenges with increased resilience and clarity, ultimately promoting a more centered and balanced way of living.

Progressive muscle relaxation, or PMR, includes

methodically tensing and then relaxing various muscle groups to encourage mental and physical calm. This technique, created in the early 1900s by physician Edmund Jacobson, assists people in identifying and releasing stored stress in their bodies. PMR deepens awareness of body sensations and promotes deep relaxation by methodically contracting and releasing muscles. This method works exceptionally well for people suffering from headaches and tense muscles due to stress.

Technology and mindfulness are combined in the

biofeedback method to improve stress management. Biofeedback devices give people real-time feedback by measuring physiological factors, including skin conductance, muscle tension, and heart rate. People can learn to intentionally control their physiological reactions—such as lowering their heart rate or tensing up their muscles—by paying attention to this input. Biofeedback encourages a sense of agency in stress management by giving people more control over their physical processes.

A muscular relaxation and stress reduction technique is guided imagery, which entails the creation of vivid mental images. Under the direction of a facilitator or with the aid of recorded scripts, participants enter a happy and relaxing mental environment. Using the senses, this visualization technique takes people to a calm and peaceful state of mind. In addition to diverting from stressful situations, guided imagery lowers stress hormones and fosters inner calm by assisting in the physiological relaxation response.

Creativity and the arts provide special channels for stress relief, letting people express themselves and go on a journey of self-discovery. Art therapy offers a non-verbal way to manage emotions and lower stress levels, whether through painting, drawing, or other creative endeavors. Making art induces a meditative state that encourages mindfulness and relaxation. People can channel their emotions via artistic creation, which offers a therapeutic avenue for stress relief and self-expression.

Laughing therapy, often known as humor therapy or laughing management, is a playful yet powerful method of stress reduction. Endorphins are the body's natural feel-good chemicals that are released when you laugh, which enhances your overall feeling of wellbeing. Laughter therapy entails purposefully engaging in things that make people laugh, such as watching comedies, going to laughter yoga classes, or engaging in games. People can offset the physiological and psychological impacts of stress by including daily laughter, promoting a happy emotional state.

Yoga is a traditional form of stress relief that incorporates physical postures, breathing exercises, and meditation. It has become quite popular. Yoga combines breath, movement, and mindfulness to improve general well-being and encourage relaxation. People have various choices regarding integrating yoga into their lives, such as Hatha, Vinyasa, and Restorative yoga types. Yoga is a thorough method for stress reduction because it not only releases physical tension but also fosters emotional balance and mental focus.

The ancient Chinese martial art of tai chi has developed into a well-liked mind-body exercise known for its ability to reduce stress. Tai chi calls for deliberate, deep diaphragmatic breathing, slow, flowing movements, and mental attention. Tai Chi's soft, rhythmic style helps people unwind, regain equilibrium, and feel physically and mentally better. Tai Chi's innate awareness enables people to be fully present in every movement, which promotes calmness and resilience to stress.

Using the healing qualities of essential oils, aromatherapy helps people unwind and reduce tension. Plant-based essential oils are used in various ways, including inhalation, topical application, and diffusers. Citrus, chamomile, and lavender scents have all been linked to soothing effects on the nervous system. In addition to stimulating the sense of smell, aromatherapy improves emotional health by generating a calming, stress-relieving sensory environment.

Expressive writing is the deliberate expression of ideas and feelings via written form. It is a contemplative and therapeutic practice. People write in an organized manner, frequently concentrating on their innermost feelings and ideas regarding traumatic events. Expressing emotions through words allows people to externalize and process their experiences. Numerous psychological advantages of expressive writing have been connected, such as lowered stress levels, happier moods, and increased general wellbeing.

With origins in antiquated contemplative traditions, meditation is a flexible and well-researched method of stress reduction. There are many different types of meditation, including transcendental, loving-kindness, and mindfulness meditation. ToGuided visualization, mantra repetition, and breath awareness are standard methods utilized in meditation to cultivate a concentrated and present-moment state of mind. Frequent meditation has been linked to gains in general mental health, less stress, and enhanced emotional resilience.

Therapy (CBT) is a popular therapy approach that uses a variety of approaches to assist people in recognizing and altering thought patterns that lead to stress and unpleasant emotions. In cognitive behavioral therapy (CBT), illogical ideas are examined and contested, negative thought patterns are swapped out for more positive ones, and stress management coping mechanisms are created. Evidence-based cognitive behavioral therapy (CBT) has shown promise in treating a variety of mental health issues by highlighting the connections between ideas, feelings, and actions.

Water is used in hydrotherapy, or water-based therapy, to promote relaxation and reduce tension. Hydrotherapy spa treatments, Jacuzzi sessions, and hot baths can enhance physical and mental relaxation. Water's buoyancy relieves physical strain, and its relaxing qualities have a calming influence on the mind. People can easily include hydrotherapy, a flexible and approachable stress-reduction method, into their self-care routines.

The phrase "breathwork" refers to various deliberate breathing exercises and is essential to stress reduction. Methods for controlling and optimizing breathing patterns, which encourage relaxation and lower stress levels, include Box Breathing, 4-7-8 Breathing, and Alternate Nostril Breathing. By deliberately concentrating on breathing, one can relax the nervous system and create a link between the conscious and unconscious minds. People can utilize breathwork as a convenient and easily transportable method to improve their well-being and manage stress in various contexts.

Using music's therapeutic properties, music therapy can be used to treat mental, emotional, and physical issues. Competent music therapists assist patients in achieving particular therapeutic objectives by utilizing various musical components, including rhythm, melody, and harmony. Making music, listening to, or performing music can elicit feelings, encourage relaxation, and improve general well-being. As an adjunctive strategy to stress management, music therapy is used in various contexts, such as clinical settings, educational institutions, and community settings.

By generating a calm state of awareness, akin to meditation, self-hypnosis is a practice that can lead to a heightened degree of suggestibility. Individuals use self-guided scripts or recordings to induce a trance-like condition in which they can concentrate on visualizations and affirmations. The goal of self-hypnosis is to use the subconscious mind's ability to shape perceptions, actions, and feelings. Some studies indicate that self-hypnosis can help lower stress and enhance general mental health, but further research is required.

Frederick Matthias Alexander created the Alexander Technique, a mind-body approach that targets ingrained movement and posture patterns that can exacerbate tension and stress. This method entails teaching people how to use their bodies more effectively and synchronously again. The Alexander Technique helps people improve posture, lessen physical discomfort associated with stress, and release needless tension by encouraging awareness and mindfulness in movement. The technique's concepts can be used in various contexts, enhancing general well-being.

In summary, the variety of stress-reduction methods—such as breathing exercises, mindfulness, and other strategies—highlights the range of instruments at one's disposal for fostering calm and improving mental wellbeing. Every style provides a different viewpoint and approach, meeting the requirements and preferences of the individual. People can pick from various stress management techniques to build a unique and successful approach to wellbeing, whether through traditional practices like yoga and meditation or more modern approaches like biofeedback and music therapy. By incorporating these strategies into daily life, people can deal with the difficulties of contemporary living with more resilience, which promotes a comprehensive and long-term approach to stress management.

CHAPTER V

Transforming Negative Emotions

Alchemical Processes for Transforming Emotions

Alchemy, the age-old practice that is frequently connected to turning base metals into gold, also explores the transformation of emotions. Although alchemical concepts are generally perceived as a pseudoscientific and mystical endeavor, they actually provide fascinating insights into the human mind and the potential for emotional conversion. In this sense, alchemy takes on the metaphorical role of a furnace where feelings undergo drastic transformations.

Prima materia refers to the unprocessed, primordial material from whence all things originate. It is a fundamental idea in alchemical philosophy. In a similar vein, emotions can be viewed as an untamed, chaotic primeval power. Alchemical procedures seek to purify this prima materia emotionale, analogous to the process of extracting impurities from gold. One important alchemical method, distillation, can be understood as a metaphor for the process of distilling an emotion of its impurities and retaining only its fundamental elements. People can develop clarity and knowledge by distilling their emotions through self-awareness and introspection.

In order to purify and convert materials, the alchemical stage of calcination entails subjecting them to extreme heat. This is comparable, from an emotional perspective, to overcoming the intense challenges life throws at you. Alchemy advises accepting the heat as a chance for emotional growth rather than giving in to it. When viewed through the prism of alchemical insight, adversities become transforming events that burn away emotional dross and develop resilience and wisdom.

The coniunctio, or the joining of opposites, is a key

concept in alchemy. This alchemical marriage brings about the reconciliation of emotions, which are typically perceived as opposing forces. Instead of being a chaotic fight, the interaction of happiness and sadness, love and hate, becomes a harmonic dance. People can transcend polarities in favor of a holistic emotional experience by accepting the oneness of opposites and navigating emotional complications with a newfound equilibrium.

Emotional mastery and the alchemical search for the

philosopher's stone, a fabled material said to provide immortality, are similar. Emotional metamorphosis stands for the apex of personal development, just as the stone signifies the height of alchemical achievement. Achieving a harmonious equilibrium similar to the philosopher's stone is the first step on the path to emotional mastery: harmonizing the various facets of one's emotional landscape.

The idea of the albedo, a stage marked by illumination

and purity, is also introduced by alchemy. This corresponds to a process of introspection and awakening on an emotional level. People can attain a level of emotional clarity and remove the shadows that hide their actual sentiments by investigating and comprehending the causes of their emotions. By encouraging people to accept sincerity and vulnerability, the albedo helps people establish a strong bond with their emotional selves.

The blackening, or nigredo, represents the plunge into

the unconscious's depths. Alchemical emotional change similarly requires facing and embracing the shadow elements of emotions. Through recognizing and incorporating repressed or disregarded feelings, people traverse the depths of their minds and come out on the other side with a more complex and comprehensive picture of who they are.

To sum up, the alchemical procedures for changing feelings provide a symbolic structure for comprehending and negotiating the complexities of the human emotional experience. People go on a transforming journey toward emotional mastery and self-discovery through distillation, calcination, coniunctio, and other alchemical processes. Emotions become more than just reactions in the alchemical furnace; they become chances for development, insight, and significant inward transformation. With its philosophical foundations and symbolic vocabulary, the age-old wisdom of alchemy remains relevant today as a guidance for individuals who want to transform the basic aspects of their emotions into the gold of self-realization.

Turning Challenges into Opportunities for Growth

It is impossible to avoid encountering obstacles along the path of life. Challenges can mold our personalities and reroute our course of action, regardless of whether they originate from personal hardships, professional setbacks, or unanticipated situations. The transformational viewpoint rests in the ability to change these problems into chances for growth, even though it is simple to become demoralized when confronted with adversity.

This transformative mindset is characterized by several key elements, one of which is recognizing that challenges are not obstacles but stepping stones. Challenges should not be seen as insurmountable impediments but should be regarded as opportunities for personal and professional growth. Every obstacle presents an opportunity to gain knowledge, adjust one's approach, and emerge more powerful than one was before. When it comes to personal development, difficulties serve as the impetus for self-discovery and the development of resilience. Doing so encourages us to contemplate our capabilities, priorities, and values, resulting in a more profound comprehension of who we are.

When it comes to the business world, challenges are nothing new, and successful firms are aware that overcoming obstacles is an essential component of progress. Variations in the market, disruptions caused by technical advancements, and shifting competitive landscapes create ongoing issues. On the other hand, inventive companies view these issues not as threats but as opportunities to develop and evolve. Firms can continue to be relevant and keep a competitive edge by adapting to change, whether unavoidable or voluntary. For instance, during the COVID-19 pandemic, there was a global trend towards remote work, which drove businesses to adopt digital transformation to cultivate a work environment that was more flexible and robust.

By adopting a growth mindset, a notion popularized by psychologist Carol S. Dweck, individuals, and companies can reap the benefits of this approach. This way of thinking views difficulties not as indications of one's competencies but as opportunities to acquire new knowledge and develop oneself. Cultivating a zest for learning, perseverance in the face of failure, and perceiving effort as a road to mastery are all components of adopting a growth mindset. Not only does this attitude increase the performance of individuals, but it also fosters a culture of continual development inside businesses.

Discovering the positive aspects of a situation is crucial in transforming difficulties into opportunities. In many cases, adversity reveals latent capabilities, resiliency, and resources that have yet to be utilized. Individuals and organizations can use the time they are confronted with obstacles as an opportunity for introspection, thereby seeing capabilities that may have been overlooked under more comfortable circumstances. If a professional is experiencing a setback in their job, they may uncover new strengths in their capacity to adapt and their ability to solve problems. In a similar vein, a business that is experiencing financial difficulties may discover unrealized potential within its workers or find alternate sources of revenue.

Working together and providing support are two of the most critical factors in transforming obstacles into opportunities for personal development. When faced with difficult circumstances, seeking counsel from mentors, working with peers, or cultivating an environment that supports the team can be beneficial. These activities can provide significant insights and assistance. An innovative approach to problem-solving is facilitated by sharing experiences and considering various views, which enables individuals and organizations to handle difficulties more efficiently. When confronted with challenges, the capability of collective wisdom frequently manifests itself, so laying a more solid groundwork for future achievements.

Furthermore, transforming problems into chances for growth also requires a significant amount of resilience on the part of the individual. The ability to recover quickly from failures, adjust to new circumstances, and keep a good attitude despite challenges is essential to resilience. People who work on developing their resilience get better at overcoming obstacles and serve as a source of motivation for those around them. Resilient leaders in the corporate sector can steer their teams through turbulent times while instilling confidence and a sense of purpose in their followers.

The notion of post-traumatic growth, which was developed by psychologists Richard G. Tedeschi and Lawrence G. Calhoun, is an additional illustration of the transforming potential of going through difficult experiences. The idea behind this notion is that people who go through considerable hardship might achieve positive psychological growth due to their experiences. This process frequently results in enhanced self-awareness, a deeper appreciation for life, and the formation of new perspectives and objectives. Even though confronting obstacles is unpleasant, it often leads to these.

In addition, the ability to adapt and the growth

mentality that is developed through the process of overcoming obstacles are factors that lead to long-term success. People who can overcome the barriers and gain knowledge from them can build the abilities necessary to succeed in dynamic and unpredictable circumstances. When it comes to the world of business, organizations that choose to perceive problems as opportunities for innovation and progress are better positioned to maintain their success over the long run.

To transform obstacles into chances for progress, it is

not necessary to disregard the challenges one is confronted with; instead, it is essential to reframe one's perspective. Individuals and organizations can harness the transformative power of challenges by shifting their emphasis from the problem itself to the possibility for learning and development that the obstacle presents. It is necessary to have a mindset that places a high value on resiliency, continual learning, teamwork, and identifying the positive aspects of difficult situations to embrace adversities as growth accelerators.

In conclusion, difficulties are an inevitable component of

life, and how we make sense of them and react to them determines the course of our trip. The ability to view challenges as chances for progress rather than as things that should be avoided at all costs can lead to revolutionary outcomes. It is necessary to cultivate a growth mentality, look for the positive aspects of a situation, embrace resilience, and look for support and collaboration to complete the process. Not only can individuals and organizations negotiate obstacles more effectively by adopting this approach, but they can also emerge more robust, more resilient, and better equipped for future success. The human potential for adaptation, learning, and change is demonstrated by the voyage's trip from adversity to growth.

Building Resilience Through Emotional Transformation

Building resilience through emotional transformation is a multifaceted process encompassing the ability to adapt, bounce back from adversity, and cultivate emotional well-being. The ability to harness the strength of one's emotions to navigate the obstacles and uncertainties of life is an essential component of emotional resilience. Individuals must detect and comprehend their emotional reactions to various circumstances, which is why self-awareness is frequently the starting point of this transforming journey. Individuals can then advance towards a higher level of emotional intelligence, which paves the path for resilience if they acknowledge and embrace the emotions that they are experiencing.

In addition, developing appropriate mechanisms is necessary to increase resilience through emotional transformation. Individuals are given the ability to deal with challenges and disappointments without giving in to negative emotional states through these techniques. Within this process, techniques such as mindfulness, positive reframing, and cognitive restructuring play critical roles. People who practice mindfulness are more likely to be present at the moment, which helps them feel more at ease and lessens the impact of the things that cause them stress. Cognitive restructuring involves challenging negative thought patterns, whereas positive reframing involves adjusting viewpoints to uncover possibilities for development and learning inside challenges.

Additionally, developing a robust support network is an essential component of creating resilience. Emotional transformation is not a journey that can be undertaken in isolation; instead, it flourishes when social connections accompany it. A solid basis for emotional well-being is provided by healthy connections, which bring support, understanding, and a sense of belonging to the individual inside the relationship. Through connecting with others, individuals can share their experiences, acquire new perspectives, and receive encouragement while going through challenging circumstances. Through the reinforcement of a sense of community and common humanity, this social support, in turn, significantly contributes to the development of positive emotional resilience.

The practices of self-care are very intimately connected to the concept of emotional resilience. To develop resilience, it is vital to place a priority on one's physical, mental, and emotional well-being. Getting enough sleep, engaging in regular physical activity, and maintaining a good diet all contribute to overall physiological balance, which in turn has a positive impact on emotional states. Another way to improve one's emotional well-being is to participate in activities that bring happiness, relaxation, and contentment. An individual's capacity to handle obstacles with a resilient mentality is strengthened when they make a conscious effort to incorporate self-care routines into their everyday lives.

Developing a development mindset is another essential component of emotional transformation that is essential to building resilience. To build resilience, it is necessary to view adversities not as insurmountable hurdles but as chances for personal development and growth. Individuals with a growth mentality are motivated to persevere in the face of hardship and are encouraged to perceive failures as temporary barriers to progress. A shift in viewpoint like this encourages adaptation, inventiveness, and taking a proactive approach to problem-solving, which eventually contributes to increased resilience.

In addition, developing emotional control is a necessary component of creating resilience through emotional transformation. To successfully navigate the intricacies of life, it is essential to possess the ability to control and manage one's feelings. Deep breathing, gradual muscle relaxation, and mindfulness meditation are some of the techniques that enable individuals to regulate their emotional responses, so reducing the escalation of stress and anxiety. The development of these skills allows individuals to approach obstacles with a calm and serene demeanor, which in turn enhances their capacity to endure in the face of adversity.

Building resilience through emotional transformation is a dynamic and empowering process that includes self-awareness, coping mechanisms, social connections, self-care practices, a development mindset, and emotional regulation. In conclusion, this process involves all of these aspects. To face the problems that life throws at them with grace and grit, individuals are equipped with the tools and mentality necessary for this transforming journey. Through the cultivation of emotional resilience, individuals cannot only recover from failures but also flourish in the face of adversity, thereby developing a profound sense of well-being and empowerment.

CHAPTER VI

Interpersonal Emotional Intelligence

Nurturing Healthy Relationships

Nurturing healthy relationships is a cornerstone of a fulfilling and meaningful life. These relationships—whether with loved ones, close friends, or romantic partners—substantially impact one's general well-being. Good communication is essential to developing wholesome relationships. Understanding, trust, and closeness are nurtured by transparent and honest communication. It entails not just expressing oneself but also paying attention to what others say, appreciating their viewpoints, and acknowledging their feelings. This mutually beneficial exchange builds a basis for stronger relationships and a sense of respect and support.

Furthermore, empathy and compassion are the foundation of solid partnerships. Relationships that endure hardship and the passage of time are forged by empathy and sharing in the emotions of others. Empathy promotes emotional connection and a feeling of being fully seen and heard by enabling people to connect more deeply. Relationships are strengthened by compassion, which is sincere care for the welfare of others. Kindness, tolerance, and a readiness to help one another through successes and setbacks are encouraged.

Another essential component of fostering wholesome relationships is boundaries. Setting and upholding limits is crucial to preserving personal freedom and creating a secure environment in a partnership. Defined limits help to avoid misunderstandings and confrontations by establishing a framework for respect for one another. Healthy partnerships recognize the value of striking a balance between intimacy and personal space so that each partner can continue to be a supportive member of the relationship while preserving their individuality and pursuing personal development.

The foundation of any successful relationship is trust.

Integrity, dependability, and consistency are necessary for establishing and preserving trust. Since trust is brittle, it might be difficult to regain once lost. Honesty and openness are, therefore, crucial. People in good relationships place a high value on being trustworthy and create an atmosphere that fosters trust. Vulnerability, sharing one's true self, and knowing that one can rely on one's partner or loved ones in difficult times are all made possible by trust.

Furthermore, cultivating gratitude and respect for others reinforces the foundation of wholesome relationships. Thanking the other person for all the tiny and significant positive parts of the relationship strengthens the emotional bond. A culture of affirmation and acknowledgment is created by showing appreciation for the distinct traits and accomplishments that each partner brings to the partnership. Acknowledging and expressing thanks produces a positive feedback loop that encourages a friendly, amiable, and supportive environment.

Another essential component of fostering strong relationships is cultivating common values and objectives. Even if each person may have different interests and goals, coming together to share something familiar gives them a sense of purpose and solidarity. Aligning aspirations, whether through shared beliefs, interests, or long-term objectives, fosters a sense of cooperation. A sense of companionship and shared purpose are fostered in healthy relationships by supporting each other's personal development and cooperating to achieve common goals.

The ability to resolve conflicts is essential to the survival of partnerships. Arguments will inevitably arise, but how they are resolved determines how strong the bond is. When there is a disagreement, healthy couples aim to understand instead of place blame. Active listening, empathy, and a dedication to working together to discover solutions are necessary for effective conflict resolution. People in healthy relationships view disagreements as chances for personal development and education because they know that working things out improves communication and fortifies partnerships.

In addition, promoting playfulness and enjoyment

enhances the vitality of wholesome relationships. Emotional bonds are strengthened, and happy memories are created through laughter and shared pleasure. Lightheartedness and companionship are fostered by taking delight in each other's company and indulging in enjoyable activities. A dynamic and resilient relationship is nurtured by balancing severe aspects of the relationship with lighthearted moments.

Last but not least, maintaining wholesome relationships

requires constant dedication and work. Like any other element of life, relationships demand ongoing commitment. This entails making time for each other a priority, showing love and affection daily, and adjusting to the relationship's shifting dynamics and demands. People who are in good relationships know that it takes commitment, endurance, and a readiness to change as a couple to maintain a strong and meaningful bond.

In conclusion, developing good relationships requires

constant dedication, empathetic communication, boundaries, trust, respect, and shared values, in addition to effective dispute resolution and a lighthearted attitude. Together, these components support relationships' resiliency, strength, and vibrancy, laying the groundwork for people to flourish emotionally and find fulfillment in their interactions with others. The support, happiness, and personal development of healthy relationships enhance a person's life.

Empathy and Compassion in Interpersonal Connections

Empathy and compassion are the cornerstones of meaningful and fulfilling interpersonal connections, weaving a tapestry of understanding, support, and shared humanity. The foundation of meaningful connection is empathy, which can be defined as the capacity to comprehend and identify with the emotions of various individuals. It requires an active effort to understand the perspective and feelings of another person, which goes beyond simple pity. Individuals who demonstrate empathy in their relationships create an environment where others feel they are being heard and validated. This kind of emotional resonance helps to cultivate a sense of proximity, which in turn helps to break down boundaries and deepen the relationships that bind individuals together.

Complementing empathy in cultivating interpersonal connections is compassion, which can be defined as a genuine concern for the well-being of other people. Not only does it require an awareness of the feelings of another individual, but it also requires a sense of obligation to mitigate their pain or contribute positively to their enjoyment. Individuals are encouraged to behave with kindness, patience, and a desire to offer support when motivated by compassion, which goes beyond self-interest. When it comes to interpersonal interactions, compassion serves as a directing force, fostering an environment that is characterized by care and regard. Furthermore, it reinforces the idea that, in our interconnected existence, the well-being of one is closely tied to the well-being of all. This is because it emphasizes that all people share the human experience of joy and agony.

Additionally, in addition to contributing to the formation of safe and supportive workplaces, understanding and compassion are also important. Trust is fostered when persons have the sense that they are understood and cared for. Once established, this trust serves as the foundation around which healthy relationships are constructed. People can feel safe expressing their genuine selves in these kinds of circumstances because they are aware that their feelings and vulnerabilities will be met with empathy and compassion rather than judgment. This feeling of security encourages open conversation and emotional closeness, which in turn enables individuals to connect on a more profound level and to form ties that will last.

Additionally, empathy and compassion are essential components in conflict resolution. Constructive discourse is made more accessible when one can empathize with the perspective of another person, particularly in situations when there is disagreement or misunderstanding. Individuals who practice empathy make it a priority to understand the underlying feelings and reasons that are driving different points of view rather than approaching confrontations with a defensive attitude. This serves as a bridge to locating work of agreement and working together to discover answers. A further softening of the edges of conflict, compassion encourages individuals to emphasize the connection over being right, which fosters reconciliation and growth.

Further, the ability to empathize and have compassion is necessary to navigate varied and heterogeneous communities successfully. The capacity to comprehend and value the various points of view in the world is becoming increasingly important as the globe continues to evolve more interconnected. Individuals who possess empathy can put themselves in the position of another person and recognize the specific difficulties and experiences that have shaped their perspective of the world. An inclusive worldview that embraces diversity and encourages togetherness is fostered by compassion, which crosses cultural barriers and fosters cultural understanding. Individuals contribute to the formation of communities that are peaceful and understanding and that cherish the complexity of human differences when they embrace empathy and compassion.

It is essential to demonstrate empathy and compassion in the field of healthcare to provide care that is centered on the patient. Culturing these qualities by healthcare personnel results in the creation in which patients have the sense that they are both seen and heard. Listening attentively to patients, acknowledging their worries and concerns, and working together to find solutions to their problems are all characteristics of compassionate medical professionals. Understanding the emotional and psychological elements of illness is an essential component of compassion in the healthcare industry, which goes beyond technical expertise. It entails treating patients with dignity and kindness, as well as a real dedication to their well-being, which ultimately improves the overall patient experience and contributes to excellent health outcomes.

Furthermore, educational settings can reap tremendous benefits from introducing empathy and compassion. Educators who exemplify these characteristics can build classroom environments where students feel supported and respected. Educators can adjust their approach by gaining an understanding of the unique talents, challenges, and perspectives of each student. This helps to create a learning environment that is both inclusive and caring. Not only does compassionate teaching require passing on information to pupils, but it also involves fostering their social and emotional growth. The cultivation of a love for learning and the development of healthy relationships between teachers and students are both directly correlated to the presence of empathy and compassion in instructional settings.

There is a correlation between empathy and compassion in the workplace and the development of a constructive and collaborative culture within the firm. These characteristics are prioritized by leaders, which in turn fosters a sense of belonging and drive among the members of the team. Empathetic leaders are aware of the challenges and strengths that their team faces, which enables them to create opportunities for both personal and professional development. Recognizing the humanity of employees, comprehending the influence that their work has on their well-being, and offering assistance to them while they are going through difficult times are all components of compassionate leadership. In these kinds of work cultures, empathy and compassion drive employee engagement, contentment, and the firm's overall success.

The development of one's emotional intelligence can be improved on an individual level through empathy and compassion. Individuals can negotiate complex social dynamics with elegance and sensitivity when they possess these abilities. The capacity to comprehend and establish a connection with other individuals on an emotional level helps to cultivate more meaningful personal relationships, contributing to a feeling of belonging and fulfillment. Also of equal significance is the cultivation of empathy and compassion toward one's own existence. When one treat themselves with the same kindness and understanding they extend to others, they practice self-compassion. This helps them become more resilient and maintain their well-being despite personal obstacles.

It can be concluded that empathy and compassion are transforming energies that elevate interpersonal connections throughout a wide range of aspects of life. They build environments conducive to understanding, trust, and support, which encourages the development of good relationships. Not only are these characteristics necessary for resolving conflicts and fostering an inclusive environment, but they also play essential roles in healthcare, education, the workplace, and the overall well-being of individuals. As society continues to develop, it is becoming increasingly important to embrace and cultivate empathy and compassion. These qualities serve as guiding lights for humanity, illuminating the route toward a future that is more interconnected and caring.

Conflict Resolution and Communication Skills

Conflict resolution and communication skills are paramount in navigating the intricate web of human interactions, both in personal relationships and professional settings. Disagreements in viewpoints, attitudes, and requirements are the root cause of conflict, an inevitable component of human relationships. The ability to successfully address and resolve disputes is contingent upon having strong communication skills. Understanding, empathy, and collaborative problem-solving are all essential components in conflict resolution, and effective communication serves asisdation for all these traits. Through communication that is both open and clear, individuals can convey their thoughts, feelings, and requirements, thereby establishing a foundation for mutual comprehension.

Active listening is a crucial component in the process of conflict resolution. Listening actively requires more than just hearing the words being spoken; it also involves fully interacting with the person who is speaking, comprehending the feelings that are being conveyed, and delivering feedback that displays complete comprehension. By actively listening to one another, individuals affirm the opinions of one another, which helps to cultivate an environment that is respectful and empathic. This fundamental communication ability creates the platform for productive discourse, which enables the identification of common ground and the development of solutions that benefit both parties.

In addition, the art of assertiveness is an essential component of effectively communicating. Individuals can firmly share their opinions and desires without infringing on the rights of others when they exhibit assertiveness, which achieves a balance between passivity and violence. Assertive communication encourages transparency and honesty, which in turn reduces the possibility of misunderstandings, which can reduce the likelihood of conflicts occurring. Individuals are given the ability to articulate their boundaries, expectations, and concerns, which results in the creation of an environment in which conflicts can be addressed proactively and collaboratively.

There is a close connection between emotional intelligence and the settlement of conflicts. Emotionally intelligent individuals identify and control their feelings while also being sensitive to the feelings of others on a personal level. By gaining an understanding of the emotional undercurrents that are present in a conflict, one can engage in communication that is more nuanced and empathic. Individuals who possess emotional intelligence can recognize the influence that emotions have on their perceptions and acts, which enables them to manage disputes with sensitivity. Through the cultivation of emotional intelligence, individuals can approach conflicts with a heightened awareness of their own emotions as well as the feelings of others, so paving the way for resolutions that are both more successful and more compassionate.

Within the area of professional life, the ability to resolve conflicts is an essential skill that has a direct influence on the culture of an organization, as well as on teamwork and production. The surroundings in which people work are highly dynamic and diverse, bringing together people from various backgrounds who have multiple personalities and work in different ways. Communication that is both effective and efficient is necessary for developing teamwork and preventing conflicts from becoming more severe. Creating a culture in which open communication is encouraged, and differences are seen as opportunities for progress rather than sources of discontent is an essential component of conflict resolution in the workplace. When a business prioritizes conflict resolution skills and provides opportunities for their development, it becomes a fertile ground for innovation, creativity, and a pleasant working environment.

Leadership is one of the most critical factors that determines how the dynamics of conflict resolution are shaped inside an organization. Influential leaders not only have excellent communication and conflict resolution abilities, but they also develop structures and policies that enable a healthy resolution of problems. They build an environment where employees feel comfortable discussing issues, provide tools for conflict resolution training, and support a culture of open discussion among employees. There is a sense of camaraderie and shared purpose that is fostered in these kinds of workplaces because disagreements are seen as problems that need to be addressed through joint efforts.

Skills in conflict resolution are instrumental in educational environments, in addition to being useful in the dynamics of the workplace. Regarding relationships and interactions, teachers, students, and administrators must manage various situations that can result in problems. Having the ability to communicate effectively is necessary to establish a learning atmosphere that is constructive and positive. The ability to manage disagreements between students, to build a culture of respect, and to provide constructive feedback that further enriches the learning experience are all capabilities that teachers who nurture excellent communication skills possess. Additionally, teaching students skills in conflict resolution equips them with tools they can take into their personal and professional lives, contributing to the student's overall social and emotional growth.

On a personal level, the ability to correctly resolve conflicts is precious in the context of maintaining good relationships. It is impossible to avoid encountering disagreements in intimate relationships; thus, the capacity to navigate these disagreements via effective communication is essential for the sustainability and lifespan of the relationship. Effective communication requires the ability to articulate oneself in a way that is easily understood, to pay attention to what the other person is saying, and to work together with the other person to find solutions that satisfy the requirements of both parties. When couples, families, and friends make communication and conflict resolution a priority, they can establish bonds that can endure the test of time, which in turn fosters deeper connections and higher levels of mutual understanding.

Conflict resolution skills are critical regarding the dynamics of the family. There are many different types of families, each with unique personalities, expectations, and modes of communication. To effectively resolve family conflicts, it is necessary to strike a delicate balance between empathy, communication, and compromise. Disagreements can be emotionally charged. Family members skilled in conflict resolution can establish an atmosphere in which every family member feels heard and respected. This helps to develop the link between the family members and contributes to a living arrangement that is also harmonious.

In addition, the development of technology has introduced new aspects to the processes of communication and the resolution of conflicts. Digital communication platforms, even though they offer ease, also bring obstacles in the form of the possibility of misinterpretation and the rapid escalation of confrontations. At this point, one of the most important aspects of conflict resolution is the ability to communicate effectively within written and virtual formats. To successfully traverse the complexities of digital communication, individuals need to be aware that the tone and intent of their messages may be interpreted differently than in face-to-face discussions. The development of abilities in digital communication is essential for addressing and resolving problems in a society that is becoming increasingly interconnected and conducted virtually.

In conclusion, the ability to resolve conflicts and communicate effectively are essential components of successful interpersonal interactions, whether in a personal or professional relationship. Effective communication creates the framework for understanding, empathy, and collaboration, which in turn makes it easier to resolve issues. When individuals prioritize and hone these talents, they contribute to the formation of environments that are constructive, collaborative, and harmonious. This is true whether they are in the business, educational settings, or personal connections (personal relationships). It is becoming increasingly clear that cultivating effective conflict resolution and communication skills is becoming increasingly vital as we traverse the complexity of an interconnected world. These abilities serve as cornerstones for the development of communities that are robust, resilient, and filled with prosperity.

CHAPTER VII

Emotional Intelligence in the Workplace

The Role of Emotional Intelligence in Professional Success

Emotional intelligence (EI) has become increasingly important in the modern workplace since it significantly determines professional success and effectiveness. When compared to traditional methods of evaluating intelligence, which are primarily concerned with cognitive capabilities, emotional intelligence goes into the domain of comprehending and controlling one's own emotions as well as those of others. Self-awareness, self-regulation, empathy, motivation, and social skills are all included in this group of competencies. The function of emotional intelligence has gained prominence in defining not just individual career trajectories but also the overall effectiveness of teams and workplaces. This is because organizations increasingly recognize the value of interpersonal dynamics and teamwork.

Self-awareness is a vital component of emotional intelligence that is often overlooked. Those who are professionals and have a high level of self-awareness have a profound comprehension of their feelings, their capabilities, and their limitations, as well as how these aspects influence their conduct. Individuals can negotiate the complexity of the workplace with a precise grasp of their impact on others as we, ll as thandaadapttof scenarios when they have this kind of self-insight. When it comes to managing stress, making judgments based on accurate information, and establishing genuine connections with coworkers, clients, and superiors, self-aware professionals are better equipped.

Additionally, self-regulation, which is another component of emotional intelligence, is an essential component in the achievement of professional success. Individuals who possess good self-regulation skills can control and redirect feelings and urges that are disruptive. When it comes to the working world, the capacity to keep one's calm under pressure, to deal with failures gracefully, and to maintain one's concentration on long-term objectives is extraordpreciouse of the dynamic and fast-paced nature of today's workplaces, professionals who succeed in self-regulation are frequently regarded as adaptive and resilient. These are characteristics that contribute significantly to the process of navigating these environments.

Empathy, which may be defined as the ability to comprehend and identify with the emotions of other people, is an essential component of emotional intelligence that has far-reaching implications for the achievement of professional goals. Professionals who exhibit empathy are sensitive to the requirements and points of view of their coworkers, clients, and team members. This capacity helps to cultivate healthy relationships, facilitates practical cooperation, and enables individuals to traverse varied and multicultural work situations successfully. When it comes to leadership responsibilities, empathy is potent because it allows leaders to connect with their teams on a deeper level, which in turn inspires trust and commitment from their followers.

When discussing emotional intelligence, the term "motivation" refers to the capacity to propel oneself toward the achievement of one's goals and to persevere in the face of temporary or permanent failures. The professionals who are highly driven are not only enthusiastic about their work, but they are also able to remain resilient in the face of difficulties. A commitment to continual growth, a readiness to take on additional duties, and a good influence on the team's morale are all fueled by this intrinsic motivation. Motivated people frequently demonstrate a strong work ethic and the capacity to inspire and motivate those around them, which contributes to an environment at work that is both good and productive.

Emotional intelligence comprises several dimensions, the ultimate one being social skills, which encompass various characteristics essential for successful relationships with other people. The ability to communicate effectively, resolve conflicts, and establish and sustain relationships are all areas where professionals with excellent social skills flourish. Particularly important in group situations, when effective communication and teamwork are essential to accomplishing shared objectives, these skills are critical. People with strong social skills can establish work settings that are welcoming and encouraging, which helps collaboration and shared achievement.

Regarding leadership responsibilities, the value of emotional intelligence becomes even more apparent. When it comes to understanding and controlling their own emotions, as well as detecting and responding to the feelings of others, leaders who possess a high level of emotional intelligence are highly skilled; because of this deep understanding, leaders can make decisions that take into consideration the well-being of their team members, which results in a leadership style that is both positive and inclusive. In addition, emotionally intelligent leaders can manage intricate interpersonal dynamics, successfully settle disagreements, and motivate their teams to achieve remarkable achievements.

When it comes to developing cohesive and high-performing groups, emotional intelligence is a factor that helps the success of team settings. Generally speaking, teams that are made up of individuals who have a high level of emotional intelligence tend to demonstrate improved communication, teamwork, and adaptability.

Members have an understanding of and respect for one another's points of view, which contributes to a more peaceful and productive working environment. Furthermore, emotionally intelligent teams are better ready to traverse obstacles because members can successfully manage disagreements, support one another during stressful moments, and maintain a shared focus on organizational goals. This makes emotionally intelligent teams better suited to face challenges.

Organizations that make emotional intelligence a priority within their culture typically experience significant increases in their level of success. There is a correlation between a workplace that highly emphasizes emotional intelligence and cultivates it and greater levels of employee morale, engagement, and retention. Furthermore, teams within such businesses can better adapt to change, have improved problem-solving capacities, and are exceptionally skilled at utilizing diversity to propel innovation. Emotional intelligence has a beneficial impact that extends beyond the performance of an individual, as it has the power to influence the environment of an organization as a whole and contribute to the success and sustainability of an organization over the long term.

On the other hand, despite the apparent significance of the topic, cultivating emotional intelligence in the workplace is not without difficulties. In many professional contexts, the emphasis has typically been placed on technical skills and cognitive abilities. As a result, emotions' crucial role in decision-making, teamwork, and overall job performance is sometimes overlooked. Organizations are becoming more aware of the need for emotional intelligence training and development programs to fill this void in their human resources departments. To cultivate a more emotionally intelligent workforce, these efforts intend to improve employees' understanding of themselves, their ability to interact with others, and their general emotional intelligence.

In addition, the incorporation of emotional intelligence evaluations into hiring new employees and evaluating their performance is becoming increasingly frequent. It is common knowledge among employers that assessing an applicant's emotional intelligence throughout the recruiting process can result in improved dynamics within a team and a more cohesive culture inside the firm. Evaluating an individual's capacity to cooperate, lead, and positively contribute to the workplace may provide significant insights, and analyzing an individual's emotional intelligence during performance reviews can also provide valuable information.

It is indisputable that emotional intelligence plays a significant part in professional success. To successfully navigate the intricacies of the modern workplace, it is essential to possess this comprehensive skill set, which includes self-awareness, self-regulation, empathy, motivation, and social skills. Not only do professionals who have a high emotional intelligence perform exceptionally well on their own, but they also make a significant contribution to the accomplishments of their teams and companies. Emotional intelligence training is vital to achieving sustained professional success in today's dynamic and linked professional landscape. This is because workplaces are evolving to emphasize the importance of cooperation, adaptability, and positive interpersonal dynamics.

Leadership and Emotional Intelligence

Leadership is not limited to managing duties and making strategic decisions; it encompasses much more. Additionally, it delves into the realm of feelings and the complexities of interpersonal relationships, going beyond the concrete parts of the function entirely. Within the framework of this discussion, the idea of emotional intelligence (EI) has arisen as an essential component in determining what constitutes effective leadership. The term "emotional intelligence" refers to the capacity to identify, comprehend, and control one's feelings, as well as the capacity to perceive and influence other people's feelings. The importance of emotional intelligence in the formation of great leaders is becoming more apparent than ever as the nature of leadership continues to grow more intricate and interwoven.

Self-awareness is considered one of the most critical aspects of emotional intelligence. People in leadership positions with a high level of self-awareness are aware of their feelings, strengths, flaws, and impact on others. Leaders can tackle difficulties with a clear understanding of their perspectives and prejudices when they have this level of self-awareness. It enables them to make decisions that are not just rational but also emotionally intelligent, taking into consideration the sentiments and well-being of their team members. A self-aware leader is better suited to deal with stress, maintain composure in difficult circumstances, and demonstrate a leadership style that is consistent and authentic.

Alongside self-awareness, self-regulation is another essential component of emotional intelligence in leadership. Self-regulation is a crucial component of it. Managing and controlling one's emotions, impulses, and reactions is essential for self-regulation. Leaders who can hold their feelings are less likely to be swayed by fleeting disappointments or unsuccessful attempts at achieving their goals. Instead, they can keep calm and collected, giving their troops a sense of consistency and stability. Maintaining this emotional stability during times of uncertainty or transition is essential since it contributes to creating a working environment that is conducive to productivity and innovation for employees.

On the other hand, the breadth of emotional intelligence goes beyond the self-awareness and management of an individual within themselves. A highly effective leader is also skilled at identifying and comprehending the feelings that other people are experiencing. Because of this social awareness, leaders can empathize with the people of their team, which facilitates the development of a sense of connection and trust. Putting oneself in the position of another person, comprehending their point of view, and responding with sensitivity are all essential components of empathy, which is a fundamental component of emotional intelligence. Leaders who exhibit empathy are responsible for creating a healthy and supportive workplace culture in which employees feel appreciated and understood.

In addition, effective leadership necessitates the ability to manage relationships, which can be defined as the capacity to navigate and positively impact other people's feelings. People in leadership positions who are skilled in relationship management can construct and sustain good relationships within their teams and throughout the corporation. They can communicate effectively, address disagreements with tact and diplomacy, and motivate others to work together. In addition to contributing to a more engaged and motivated workforce, a leader skilled in relationship management can cultivate a sense of togetherness and camaraderie among their employees.

Emotional intelligence influences leadership in several dimensions of a company's performance. One crucial aspect is the level of employee involvement. Leaders with a high level of emotional intelligence can create an atmosphere at work that encourages employees to be engaged and committed to their tasks. These leaders understand and address their team members' emotional needs, which helps cultivate a feeling of purpose and belonging among their associates. When employees perceive that their leaders care about their well-being and growth, they are more likely to be motivated and dedicated to their work.

Furthermore, good communication is a foundational component of successful leadership, and emotional intelligence is vital in maintaining that communication. Emotionally intelligent individuals can effectively communicate their messages in a way that is both clear and compassionate. Because of this, they know the significance of nonverbal cues, tone, and timing in the communication process. By adapting their mode of communication to their audience's emotional requirements, these leaders can establish trust and connection with their followers. It is vital to communicate in a way that is both clear and empathic to successfully align members of a team with the goals of the company, navigate change, and resolve conflicts.

The development of high-performing teams is facilitated by emotional intelligence, which plays a role in the dynamics of teams. Building a culture of cohesiveness and collaboration within a team is possible for leaders who can comprehend and control the feelings of individual team members. As a result of their recognition and appreciation of the various abilities and views within their teams, they can capitalize on these distinctions to innovate and solve problems. A leader with a high level of emotional intelligence can cultivate an environment that is welcoming to all members of the team, ensures that they are appreciated and cherished, and inspires them to make their best efforts.

The connection between emotional intelligence and successful leadership becomes apparent when a crisis occurs. Leaders who can negotiate their own emotions and sympathize with the concerns of their team members are better suited to direct their organizations through uncertain situations. This is especially true when the conditions are challenging. Leaders with high emotional intelligence can display emotional resilience, which serves as a source of inspiration for their teams. This, in turn, instills confidence and a determination to accomplish something.

The growth and nurturing of emotional intelligence are ongoing processes, even though the value of emotional intelligence in leadership is generally recognized.

Leaders can improve their emotional intelligence by self-reflecting, receiving feedback, and intentional practice. Establishing a culture that places a premium on emotional intelligence is also essential. Organizations can develop training programs, mentorship initiatives, and leadership development opportunities centered on the cultivation of abilities related to emotional intelligence. Organizations can ensure that their leaders are well-equipped to manage the complexity of the modern workplace if they emphasize emotional intelligence as a component of leadership development.

In conclusion, leadership and emotional intelligence are inextricably linked, with emotional intelligence being crucial in determining leadership effectiveness. A high level of self-awareness, self-regulation, social awareness, and the ability to manage relationships are all abilities that successful leaders possess. They are confident in their ability to utilize emotional intelligence to cultivate engagement, communication, and cooperation because they are aware of the impact of emotions on both themselves and their colleagues. The landscape of leadership is constantly shifting, and as a result, emotional intelligence is becoming increasingly crucial in developing leaders who can overcome obstacles, motivate their teams, and facilitate the success of their organizations.

Creating a Positive Emotional Climate at Work

The workplace is not only a location for carrying out activities and meeting deadlines; it is a dynamic setting in which human emotions play a fundamental part in forming the ambiance as a whole. There has been a growing realization among organizations of the tremendous impact that emotions have on their employees' well-being, engagement, and productivity. This has led to the concept of a positive emotional environment at work, which has garnered increasing prominence. When cultivating a positive emotional climate, it is not enough to be joyful on the surface; it is also necessary to establish an encouraging, compassionate, and welcoming atmosphere in which employees feel valued and motivated. The purpose of this section is to investigate the significance of fostering a pleasant emotional climate at work, the essential elements that contribute to creating such an atmosphere, and the practical benefits that such an environment delivers to both individuals and businesses.

Acknowledging the human element in the workplace is the most critical factor in fostering a pleasant emotional atmosphere. Employees are not only a machine's components; they are members of the human race who have feelings, goals, and a want to feel connected to others. Organizations and leaders who are aware of this fundamental reality recognize the significance of cultivating an environment in which employees have the sense that they are supported and acknowledged during their work. Authentic leadership is the foundation upon which this recognition is built. Authentic leaders are not just capable in their professions, but they are also compassionate and approachable. When leaders show that they genuinely care about the individuals on their team, it creates an atmosphere that is psychologically and emotionally supportive.

Communication is one of the most critical factors in the workplace that determines the emotional atmosphere. Having open and honest communication helps to cultivate trust and lowers uncertainty, which in turn contributes to a sense of psychological safety within the organization. When there is a favorable emotional environment, employees are allowed to communicate their thoughts, concerns, and ideas freely without the fear of punishment. Actively listening to others, providing constructive feedback, and speaking with empathy are all qualities that contribute to a workplace environment in which every voice is respected. Open communication like this helps cultivate a sense of belonging and connection, both of which are vital components in developing a positive emotional climate.

The encouragement of teamwork and collaboration is another essential component of an emotionally healthy environment or atmosphere. Employees' sense of purpose and engagement are both increased when they have the impression that they are a part of a team that is supportive of them. Through recognizing and appreciating individual contributions, cultivating a culture of mutual respect, and providing chances for teamwork, leaders can enable collaboration in their organizations. An emotionally supportive environment encourages employees to share their knowledge, skills, and ideas, which ultimately results in increased innovation and problem-solving within the firm.

One of the most critical components of a solid emotional climate is inclusivity. For a workplace to be considered inclusive, diversity must be valued and ensured that every employee, regardless of their identity or origin, is made to feel respected and included. Through the creation of a sense of fairness and equality, organizations that emphasize inclusion contribute to the development of a positive emotional climate in which individuals have the sensation that they can be themselves. There are many different types of inclusive practices, such as diverse recruiting initiatives and the creation of rules that encourage work-life balance. Leaders who advocate for inclusiveness lay the groundwork for a working environment in which employees have the sense that they are accepted, respected, and empowered.

Powerful forces such as recognition and gratitude can significantly influence a positive emotional atmosphere. Employees are more likely to thrive when their efforts are recognized, and their accomplishments are taken into celebration. When leaders make a concerted effort to acknowledge and demonstrate appreciation for the contributions made by their team members, they foster an environment that is characterized by gratitude and happiness. It is possible to show gratitude in various ways, from formal awards to straightforward expressions of thanks during team meetings. Through the reinforcement of a sense of value and accomplishment, acknowledging employees' efforts, regardless of the manner, contributes to developing a positive emotional climate.

Moreover, a pleasant emotional climate is intimately linked to the employees' well-being. Organizations that prioritize the mental and emotional well-being of their staff members are able to cultivate an atmosphere in which individuals can flourish. Providing support services, encouraging a healthy balance between work and personal life, and actively addressing sources of stress within the workplace are all components of this. Leaders who prioritize the well-being of their employees convey a strong message that the firm appreciates its people not only as contributors to the bottom line but also as individuals who have holistic needs.

Another essential component in fostering a pleasant emotional climate at work is the ability to be flexible. A pleasant dynamic environment can be contributed to by providing flexible work arrangements. This is done in recognition of the fact that individuals have their specific requirements and situations. This flexibility may include the ability to work from home, flexible working hours, or modifying work schedules to accommodate individual preferences wherever possible. Leaders who prioritize flexibility express their dedication to the well-being of all their employees and recognize the significance of maintaining a healthy balance between their personal and professional lives.

The ability to resolve conflicts becomes an essential talent when it is applied within the context of a positive emotional climate. How conflicts are resolved can considerably impact the dynamic environment of the workplace. Conflicts are unavoidable in any company. Leaders who approach disagreements with a mindset that is both constructive and empathic can transform difficult circumstances into opportunities for personal development. To contribute to a workplace environment that acknowledges and addresses differences in a manner that promotes understanding and collaboration, it is essential to establish a culture that supports open communication and provides resources for conflict resolution.

The benefits of developing a positive emotional climate extend beyond the enjoyment of employees; they have measurable impacts on the firm's performance. It is likely that employees who are engaged in their work and content with their jobs will be productive, innovative, and committed to the firm's success. There is a correlation between a pleasant emotional climate and better levels of staff retention, reducing the expenses associated with employee turnover and ensuring the continuity of institutional knowledge. To add insult to injury, businesses with a favorable emotional climate are more likely to become employers of choice, which is a significant advantage in today's competitive employment market.

One such area in which the influence of a pleasant emotional climate is readily apparent is customer satisfaction. When employees have the sense that they are valued and supported, they are more likely to give good service to customers. When it comes to relationships with clients and consumers, the good feelings created within the organization automatically extend to those encounters. When employees are happy and involved in their work, they become ambassadors for the business, spreading the organization's core values and helping to build a favorable reputation in the community.

A positive emotional climate at work is a multifaceted activity that involves conscious efforts from leaders and organizations. In conclusion, this attempt demands a healthy, vibrant environment at work. Recognition of the human element in the workplace, encouragement of open communication, promotion of teamwork and collaboration, prioritization of inclusivity, provision of recognition and appreciation, prioritization of employee well-being, provision of flexibility, and development of effective strategies for conflict resolution are all components of this approach. A positive emotional climate has several benefits that extend beyond the well-being of individuals to the performance of a business. These benefits impact employee engagement, retention, customer satisfaction, and organizational success. Organizations that prioritize a positive emotional climate create a more fulfilling work environment and position themselves for sustained success in the ever-changing landscape of the modern workplace. This is especially important in a world where the lines between professional and personal life are becoming increasingly blurred.

CHAPTER VIII

Cultivating Emotional Intelligence in Children

The Importance of Early Emotional Education

It is becoming increasingly apparent that academic achievement alone is insufficient to indicate a child's overall development, so the educational landscape is constantly shifting. As a result of the realization that emotional intelligence is an essential component of personal development, educators and parents are increasingly focusing their attention on the emotional well-being of children. It has become increasingly apparent that early dynamic education, which emphasizes the development of children's emotional intelligence from an early age, is an essential component of holistic education. Within the scope of this section, the significance of early dynamic education is investigated, with a particular focus on its influence on the cognitive development, social skills, and long-term well-being of children.

Recognizing that feelings are a normal and essential component of the human experience is the fundamental principle underpinning early emotional education. Children learn to traverse a complicated world of feelings at a very young age, beginning with happiness and enthusiasm and progressing to frustration and grief. In the context of early emotional education, the goal is to equip children with the skills necessary to comprehend, communicate, and effectively control their feelings. Early inspirational literacy instruction lays the groundwork for children to cultivate a healthy relationship with their feelings, creating emotional intelligence that will serve them throughout their lives. This is accomplished by educators who introduce emotional literacy to children at a young age.

The emotional well-being of an individual is inextricably tied to their cognitive development. The concept of early dynamic education acknowledges this interconnectedness and emphasizes the function that emotions play in the formation of neural processes. Children are more likely to display excellent problem-solving skills, heightened creativity, and improved cognitive flexibility when they are emotionally aware and capable. When teachers incorporate emotional education into the curriculum, they create an atmosphere that not only encourages intellectual development but also helps students develop the ability to deal with feelings of emotional distress. Children are provided with the mental and emotional tools essential for navigating the difficulties of the current world through implementing this holistic and comprehensive approach to education.

A further point to consider is that early emotional education is essential to social development. There is a strong correlation between the capacity to comprehend and control one's feelings and the development of healthy relationships with other people. Children who have developed their emotional literacy can better sympathize with their classmates, communicate effectively, and handle the challenges they face in social situations. The development of these social skills is necessary for the establishment of good relationships, the resolution of problems, and the working together with other people. Educators make a significant contribution to the development of socially competent persons who can thrive in various social circumstances by including social and emotional learning in early schooling.

During the first few years of a kid's life, the brain goes through a period of fast development, during which neural connections are formed. These connections enable the child to learn and behave in the future. Early emotional education uses this crucial era, understanding that the brain's architecture is shaped by the events experienced emotionally. The presence of positive emotional experiences triggers the release of neurotransmitters that improve memory, attention, and learning. On the other hand, prolonged exposure to stress or unpleasant dynamic events might hinder the development of cognitive abilities. In early education, educators can contribute to building a favorable emotional climate that maximizes the brain's capacity for learning and cognitive development by emphasizing the emotional well-being of their students.

Regarding the development of emotional intelligence in early childhood, emotional regulation is strongly connected to the learning process. Children may have difficulty adequately managing their feelings because of their innate tendency to act on impulses. Children who receive early emotional education are equipped with the skills necessary to identify and control their emotions, which in turn helps them develop emotional resilience. Children develop the dynamic tools needed for navigating the problems they will face when they learn how to deal with negative emotions such as frustration, disappointment, or rage in a natural and healthy way. Children who develop this emotional resilience contribute to their mental well-being and better prepare themselves to deal with the challenges they will face as they move through the different stages of their lives.

Furthermore, the issue of emotional expression is addressed through the process of early dynamic education. It can be difficult for children to express their emotions, resulting in frustration and possible behavioral problems. Educators who incorporate dynamic education into their teaching methodology equip students with a vocabulary that allows them to communicate their feelings constructively. Because of this improved emotional vocabulary, children can articulate their feelings more effectively, reducing the possibility that they would hide their emotions or express them inappropriately. Educators significantly contribute to the development of emotionally literate persons by cultivating an atmosphere in which feelings are recognized and said in a manner that benefits the individual.

The effects of early emotional education are not limited to the confines of the school sphere. During their development into teenagers and adults, the emotional intelligence that is developed during children's formative years impacts their personal and professional lives. Individuals with high emotional intelligence are better suited to traverse the intricacies of relationships, effectively work in team situations, and make educated judgments that consider both intellectual and emotional elements. Emotional intelligence is widely acknowledged as a vital skill in business, particularly in leadership, communication, and conflict resolution. This is very important in the workplace.

Early emotional education can prevent behavioral and mental health problems, which also plays a preventive role in the process. Educators contribute to the prevention of emotional issues and behavioral challenges by providing students with the skills necessary to comprehend and control their feelings. According to the findings of several studies, those who have high emotional intelligence are less likely to suffer from mental health conditions such as anxiety, depression, and other conditions. Establishing a foundation for mental well-being and laying the groundwork for a better and more resilient adult life can be accomplished through early treatments emphasizing emotional education.

In addition, the significance of early emotional education is emphasized when seen in the context of a world that is constantly evolving and linked. Children in today's society are subjected to a wider variety of stimuli. They are confronted with a broader range of obstacles, which necessitate academic competence and emotional fortitude. An essential characteristic is the ability to negotiate uncertainty, adapt to change, and communicate effectively across various cultural and social contexts. Children are provided with the tools necessary to flourish in this intricate environment through the implementation of early emotional education. This helps cultivate a generation of individuals who are academically capable, emotionally savvy, and socially comfortable.

The significance of early emotional education cannot be stressed when it comes to the overall growth and development of children. Acknowledging the mutually beneficial relationship between emotional well-being, cognitive development, and social competence goes beyond the conventional academic learning that is typically observed. The basis for emotional intelligence is laid by early dynamic education, which equips

Practical Strategies for Parents and Educators

Parenting and education are complex and dynamic realms, each playing a pivotal role in shaping the development of children. It is necessary to have a varied arsenal of ways to support growth, well-being, and academic performance to navigate the responsibilities of parenthood or teaching careers successfully. Implementing practical tactics emphasizing communication, empathy, and positive reinforcement can create a supportive environment for children, even though a universally applicable approach has yet to be implemented. The purpose of this section is to examine practical tactics that both parents and educators may utilize. It emphasizes the significance of working together, maintaining consistency, and taking a holistic approach to foster children's overall development.

Communication that is both effective and efficient is an essential component of both parenting and education. Establishing open lines of communication with children and providing them with an atmosphere in which they are comfortable expressing their views, concerns, and feelings is a responsibility that falls on both parents and educators. To do this, parents should make it a point to actively listen to their children, ask questions with open- ended responses, and cultivate a trustworthy environment. When it comes to education, teachers should allow students to express themselves by providing venues to do so and encouraging them to talk about their experiences and viewpoints. When it comes to understanding and meeting the requirements of children, nonverbal indicators, such as body language and facial expressions, play a significant role. Effective communication goes beyond spoken conversations.

A talent extremely valuable in parenting and education is the ability to empathize with others. Cultivating a sense of connection and trust in children can be accomplished by understanding and acknowledging their feelings and opinions. Parents who exhibit empathy can create an emotionally supportive home atmosphere, recognizing their children's feelings and assisting them in navigating problems. Similarly, teachers who demonstrate empathy for their pupils can cultivate a constructive and welcoming atmosphere within the classroom. Creating a learning environment that is more engaging and motivated for kids can be accomplished by recognizing and meeting the emotional needs of the pupils.

Regarding parenting and schooling, consistency is one of the most critical factors. The circumstances in which children are raised should be consistent and predictable for them to flourish. Children can feel comfortable and comprehend boundaries better when offered consistent routines and expectations. Establishing consistent sleep routines, feeding schedules, and disciplinary measures by parents can provide a framework that enhances the development of a feeling of order in their children. It is beneficial for teachers to keep regular standards and expectations in the classroom. This helps create an atmosphere in which students know what to anticipate and how to handle their academic obligations. Not only does consistency assist children in developing self-discipline, but it also contributes to creating a sound and structured atmosphere that benefits their well-being through support.

Children's behavior can be effectively guided and motivated through a powerful approach known as favorable reinforcement. One way to encourage desirable actions and foster a pleasant learning environment is through positive reinforcement, which parents and educators may utilize. It is necessary to recognize and reward efforts, accomplishments, and positive conduct to accomplish this. It is possible to reinforce the relationship between positive actions and outcomes through positive reinforcement, which verbal praise, material prizes, or a system of privileges can accomplish. When parents and teachers pay attention to the good parts of children's behavior, they can instill a sense of self-assurance, competence, and intrinsic motivation in their children.

An approach to child development that takes a holistic perspective acknowledges that academic achievement is simply one aspect of a kid's overall development. Parents and teachers must prioritize providing their children with a well-rounded education that includes social, emotional, and physical development. The promotion of a healthy lifestyle, the development of social skills, and the encouragement of involvement in extracurricular activities are all components that contribute to a comprehensive effort. In a constantly evolving world, children need to possess a wide range of skills that go beyond academic knowledge. Parents and educators play a significant role through their guidance when it comes to encouraging children to develop resilience, flexibility, and interpersonal skills that will serve them in all facets of their lives.

Collaboration between parents and educators is essential to provide children with a constant and helpful setting. A powerful relationship is created when there are open communication channels and a shared commitment to the health and happiness of a child. Parents ought to take an active role in interacting with instructors, attending conferences between teachers and parents, and participating in school events. Additionally, it is beneficial for educators to be aware of their pupils' family background and to work with the parents to address each student's specific needs and difficulties. This collaborative method fosters a sense of continuity in the children's development, which guarantees that children receive continuous direction and support at home and in the classroom setting.

For parenting and education to be successful, it is vital to tailor techniques to each kid's specific requirements and learning styles on an individual basis. Every child is unique, possessing their own set of preferences, strengths, and shortcomings. A flexible and individualized strategy is required to acknowledge and accommodate these particular characteristics. Through careful observation and comprehension of their children's interests, learning styles, and areas of difficulty, parents should modify their parenting practices based on these findings. In the classroom, teachers should use various instructional strategies and offer varied instruction to cater to the specific requirements of each student. Parents and teachers can establish an atmosphere that is conducive to the development and education of children by applying tactics that are tailored to the specific characteristics of each child.

It is a fundamental method that helps parents and educators establish an atmosphere conducive to a kid's success. Setting reasonable expectations is one of the strategies. Having expectations that are not realistic can result in feelings of tension, irritation, and a sense of inadequacy. It is essential for parents to acknowledge and value their children's unique skills and establish objectives that align with the stage of development they are now in. To ensure that the goals for academic performance, behavior, and involvement are attainable and realistic for each student, teachers should convey these objectives clearly and concisely. Parents and teachers may help children develop a positive outlook and a sense of accomplishment by creating an encouraging environment with expectations that are within their reach.

It is an approach that goes beyond the conventional educational paradigm to encourage students to develop a passion for getting knowledge. Parents and teachers should encourage their children to learn in a way driven by their natural curiosity, emphasizing the pleasure and contentment that come from acquiring new information. To accomplish this, it is necessary to provide children with a wide range of educational opportunities, cultivate a growth mentality open to overcoming obstacles, and encourage a feeling of intrinsic desire. At the same time that teachers can introduce creative and interactive teaching approaches into the classroom, parents can participate in activities at home that encourage discovery and curiosity in their children. Parents and teachers can create the groundwork for a lifelong intellectual curiosity and personal development journey by nurturing a love of learning in their children.

The conclusion is that realistic techniques for parents and educators are multidimensional, emphasizing good communication, empathy, consistency, positive reinforcement, and a holistic approach to the development of children. Components vital to this toolbox include collaboration between educators and parents, adapting to each individual's specific requirements, setting attainable expectations, and developing a love of learning. Incorporating these tactics by parents and educators helps to create an atmosphere that is nurturing and supportive, which in turn supports the general well-being and development of children. Regarding parenting and education, the foundation of a holistic and efficient approach is the collaboration between parents and educators. This partnership is founded on a mutual commitment to the development and achievement of each child.

Building Emotional Resilience in Children

The emotional resilience of a child is a critical thread that weaves through experiences, challenges, and victories in the rich tapestry that is the development of a child during their formative years. Children who have developed emotional resilience are better equipped to deal with the inevitable highs and lows that are a part of life. Emotional resilience can be defined as the capacity to adapt, recover from adversity, and negotiate the intricacies of emotions. The cultivation of emotional resilience in children emerges as a vital part of nurturing well-being and future success in a world that is always changing and where the landscape of childhood is distinguished by a variety of influences and pressures. Through an examination of the elements that contribute to the development of emotional resilience in children, as well as the tactics that parents, educators, and caregivers can utilize to cultivate this crucial attribute, this section investigates the significance of fostering emotional resilience in children.

It is during the formative years of a child's life that the groundwork for emotional resilience is established. Emotional relationships are formed between infants and the people who care for them, which leads to the development of a sense of trust and security in their surroundings. The emotional resilience of a child is significantly influenced by the bonds that the youngster forms at a young age. The establishment of a healthy attachment with a primary caregiver offers a kid a secure and supportive foundation from which they can explore the world and learn to manage their feelings. The field of developmental psychology has conducted research that highlights the significant influence that early interactions have on the development of emotional resilience. This research also highlights the role that responsive caregiving has in the process of constructing a child's capacity to govern their emotions and deal with stress.

When it comes to the development of emotional resilience, parental participation is of the utmost importance. Children's perceptions of the world and their capacity to deal with difficulties are mostly shaped by their parents, who act as the key influencers and role models in their lives. In order to provide children with a stable emotional foundation, responsive parenting, which is characterized by warmth, attentiveness, and constant support, is particularly beneficial. It is possible for parents to help develop emotional resilience in their children by acknowledging and validating their feelings, providing comfort to their children when they are experiencing distress, and encouraging autonomy within a secure environment. Parents are able to teach their children crucial lessons in coping tactics and strategies for emotional regulation by navigating the ups and downs of their emotions alongside their children.

Within the framework of conventional educational institutions and classrooms, teachers play a crucial part in the development of emotional resilience in their students. Children are given the opportunity to connect with one another, work together, and face obstacles within the context of the school setting, which functions as a miniature version of the greater world. The development of emotional resilience can be approached in a methodical manner through the implementation of social and emotional learning (SEL) programs, which are included in the school curriculum. The development of self-awareness, social awareness, responsible decision-making, self-management, and relational skills are the primary focuses of these programs. Teachers are able to make a positive contribution to the emotional well-being of their students by incorporating social and emotional learning (SEL) into the educational framework. This provides students with the vital tools they need to navigate both academic and life obstacles.

The formation of a growth mindset is an essential component in the process of creating emotional resilience inside an individual. Dweck, a psychologist, is the one who came up with the term "growth mindset," which refers to the concept that one's capabilities and intelligence can be improved by the application of work, perseverance, and learning. Children who have a growth mentality see issues not as insurmountable hurdles but rather as chances for learning and development. Parents and teachers can inculcate a growth mindset in their children by applauding work and perseverance rather than intrinsic ability, encouraging a love for learning and highlighting the importance of resilience in the face of challenges. The adoption of a growth mindset not only improves academic performance but also makes a substantial contribution to the development of emotional resilience.

One of the most important aspects of developing emotional resilience in children is teaching them good coping mechanisms. Rather than protecting children from any and all forms of stress, parents and teachers can assist children in the development of coping techniques that will allow them to handle and progress through difficult situations. Through the use of techniques such as meditation and deep breathing exercises, practitioners of mindfulness can develop the ability to regulate their emotions. Developing children's self-awareness and communication abilities can be accomplished by encouraging them to express their feelings through the mediums of art, journaling, or discussion. It is possible for parents and teachers to enable children to confront problems with resilience by teaching them that it is acceptable to experience a range of emotions and by providing them with appropriate avenues for expression.

In addition to being a key component of emotional resilience, the development of social skills occurs.

Having the capacity to create healthy relationships, communicate effectively, and successfully navigate social situations are all factors that contribute to the overall well-being of a child. Supporting the development of social skills can be accomplished by parents through the encouragement of playdates, the promotion of teamwork, and the modeling of pleasant relationships with other people. When it comes to the educational environment, cultivating a classroom culture that places a high priority on inclusiveness, empathy, and collaboration gives children the opportunity to practice and improve their social skills. Interactions with other people that are constructive not only help people become emotionally resilient but also contribute to a sense of belonging and community.

Fostering a sense of autonomy is an essential component in the process of developing emotional resilience. Children acquire a sense of agency and self-efficacy when they are given the opportunity to make choices, find solutions to challenges, and accept responsibility for their actions. Providing children with tasks that are suitable for their age, enabling them to make decisions within realistic limitations, and encouraging them to learn from their mistakes are all ways in which parents can develop autonomy in their children. In the same vein, teachers have the ability to include project-based learning, collaborative projects, and chances for decision-making inside the classroom setting. Through the cultivation of a sense of autonomy, a kid develops the capacity to confront obstacles with a proactive and self-assured perspective.

It is impossible to stress the importance of having positive role models in the process of developing emotional resilience. As living models of how to negotiate the problems that life presents, parents, instructors, and caregivers act as those examples. The ability to demonstrate a positive attitude, good coping skills, and a model of resilience in the face of adversity are all factors that contribute to a child's awareness of resilience as a valued life skill. A setting that normalizes the ups and downs of life is created when parents and educators openly relate their personal experiences of overcoming problems. This environment reinforces the concept that resilience is a process that is continuous rather than a goal that is reached at the end of the process.

In addition to this, cultivating a sense of optimism and positive thinking is an essential component of building emotional resilience. Children who are optimistic have a tendency to tackle obstacles with a can-do attitude, considering setbacks as transient and specific to a scenario rather than as a reflection of their general capabilities. The best way for parents to foster optimism in their children is to emphasize the good sides of difficult circumstances, reframe negative thinking, and encourage their children to concentrate on finding solutions rather than focusing on difficulties. A similar approach is taken by educators, who can incorporate techniques such as goal-setting exercises, positive affirmations, and reflection into the classroom setting. As children learn to face challenges with a constructive and optimistic viewpoint, parents and educators provide a significant contribution to the development of emotional resilience by encouraging the development of a positive mindset in their children.

It is of the utmost importance to acknowledge that the process of developing emotional resilience is a continuous one that progresses along with the development of a child. The obstacles that children experience get increasingly complicated as they grow, necessitating the development of coping techniques that are both adaptable and nuanced. It is important for parents and teachers to have a heightened awareness of the ever-evolving requirements of children and to adapt their support accordingly. Continuous communication, teamwork, and a shared commitment to the child's well-being and development are all necessary components in the process of establishing a culture that places a high priority on emotional resilience.

In conclusion, the process of developing emotional resilience in children is a multi-faceted endeavor that requires the combined efforts of parents, educators, and caregivers. The formation of early attachments, responsive parenting, social and emotional learning programs, a growth mindset, efficient coping mechanisms, the development of social skills, a sense of autonomy, positive role models, and the cultivation of a positive mentality are all essential components of this process. By placing emphasis on these tactics, parents and educators are able to contribute to the development of emotionally resilient individuals who are able to traverse the challenges that life presents with adaptability, resilience, and a positive perspective. Providing children with the ability to develop emotional resilience gives them the ability to face the complexities of the world with self-assurance, empathy, and the capability to continue learning and growing throughout their entire lives.

CHAPTER IX

Integrating Emotional Alchemy into Daily Life

Creating Personalized Emotional Wellness Plans

The fast pace and demands of modern life have made emotional wellness popular. Mental well-being and emotional wellness allow people to handle life's challenges, work professionally, and contribute to their communities. Personalized moving wellness plans are becoming more popular due to the unique character of emotional well-being. These customized approaches recognize that life experiences, personality, and coping methods shape emotional health. This section discusses tailored moving wellness plans, examining the factors that affect emotional wellbeing and how individuals can tailor their approach to build and sustain a resilient and pleasant mental state.

Personalized emotional wellness plans recognize that

emotional well-being is not a one-size-fits-all concept. Everyone's dynamic landscape is shaped by their unique experiences, difficulties, and capabilities. Thus, a personalized approach to emotional wellbeing respects variation and tailors tactics to individual requirements and preferences. Customized programs for emotional well-being are more holistic and lasting because they recognize emotional differences.

Self-awareness is critical to tailored emotional wellness

regimens. Self-discovery is needed to comprehend emotions, causes, and coping techniques. This entails reviewing prior events, finding emotional patterns, and determining wellbeing or distress factors. Self- awareness reveals emotional strengths and weaknesses. This insight is essential to creating successful and tailored dynamic wellness methods.

Recognizing the interconnectedness of emotional, physical, and mental health is crucial to designing tailored dynamic wellness strategies. The mind-body connection underpins holistic health. Nutrition, sleep, and exercise significantly affect mental wellness. Lifestyle choices affect emotional health. Thus, people should embrace wellbeing habits. This may include eating well, sleeping well, and doing fun, relaxing exercise. A personalized moving wellness plan incorporates these factors for a comprehensive and sustainable approach.

Given the prevalence of stress in modern life, tailored emotional wellness regimens must include stress management. Work strain, relationship issues, and outside factors cause stress. Identifying stressors, understanding stress responses, and establishing coping methods that suit personal preferences is a personalized stress management approach. This could involve mindfulness, relaxation, or creative outlets to release stress. Customizing stress management tactics helps people build resilience and overcome obstacles.

Personalized emotional health programs require emotional intelligence—the ability to perceive, comprehend, and control one's and others' emotions. Emotional intelligence involves self-awareness, self-regulation, social awareness, and relationship management. Reflective journaling, mindfulness meditation, and intentional communication boost emotional intelligence. Emotional intelligence helps people understand their emotions and navigate social interactions with empathy and competence.

Personalized emotional wellness plans also require meaningful relationships. Humans are friendly, and interactions significantly affect emotional wellbeing.

Personal planning should emphasize strong relationships with family, friends, and the community. A dynamic open communication network, trust, and support strengthens an emotional support system. This network helps during difficult times and emphasizes the value of social relationships in vibrant health.

Meditation and mindfulness are becoming powerful elements in tailored emotional wellness strategies. Mindfulness increases awareness of thoughts and emotions by focusing on the present without judgment. Meditation, deep breathing, and mindful walking can help people develop inner peace and resilience. These practices boost self-awareness, reduce stress, and improve emotional well-being.

Personalized emotional wellness plans should include activities that bring joy, fulfillment, and meaning. Activities that reflect values and interests boost emotional wellbeing. It could be hobbies, volunteering, or setting and attaining personal goals. Individuals construct a pleasant and meaningful dynamic landscape by engaging in fulfilling and purposeful activities.

Emotional wellness is dynamic and growing thus it must be acknowledged. Personal inspirational wellness programs should change with circumstances and personal progress. Regular self-assessment, reflection, and strategy adjustments keep the plan relevant and effective. Flexibility and openness to new ideas build emotional resilience.

Personalized emotional wellness plans also include expert support when needed. Psychologists, counselors, and therapists can offer advice and coping skills. Destigmatize emotional wellbeing conversations and encourage people to seek treatment without judgment. Professional help in individualized programs shows a proactive approach to vibrant health and stresses teamwork in wellbeing.

In conclusion, building tailored emotional wellness strategies needs self-awareness, a holistic approach, and constant modification. Recognizing individual experiences, lifestyle factors, stress management, emotional intelligence, meaningful connections, mindfulness, purposeful activities, and professional support is crucial. By customizing tactics, individuals can build emotional resilience, overcome adversities, and maintain positive emotional wellbeing. By adopting tailored emotional well-being, people empower themselves to live meaningful lives.

The Continuous Journey of Emotional Growth

We spend our entire lives growing emotionally. Personal experiences, relationships, and obstacles shape emotional growth, unlike physical growth, which is more predictable. This section examines the multidimensional nature of dynamic growth, its causes, and the need to foster emotional maturity throughout life.

Recognizing that emotions are dynamic and ever-changing is vital to emotional growth. From infants' delight, grief, and curiosity to adulthood's complex emotional landscapes, emotions guide our responses to the world. Emotions drive personal development as people manage relationships, obligations, and self-discovery. Understanding these feelings and responding to them with nuance and maturity is the process.

Life events shape emotional development. Love, success, and joy boost resilience and well-being. Instead, challenges, failures, and losses allow for introspection and adjustment. Positive and negative experiences build emotional resilience, helping people adapt and learn from life's diversity. Accepting both the highs and lows of life is essential to emotional growth.

Intimate and social relationships foster emotional growth. Family, friends, coworkers, and love relationships help people understand themselves more clearly. Relationships reveal strengths, weaknesses, and behavior patterns, enabling self-reflection and growth. Interactions, whether through love or conflict, strengthen emotional intelligence and empathy.

Self-awareness underpins emotional growth. Over time, one learns to recognize and comprehend emotions, motivations, and triggers. Self-awareness requires introspection, attentiveness, and a willingness to face one's light and shadow. As people grasp their emotional landscape, they see behavior patterns, beliefs, and growth opportunities. Developing self-awareness is a lifelong process.

Emotional growth occurs at different life stages. Childhood innocence and wonder lay the groundwork for emotional development. The problems of adolescence include identity exploration and emotional complexity. Adulthood brings responsibilities, relationships, and more emotions. Each life stage offers distinct dynamic growth chances, requiring individuals to adapt, learn, and mature to changing situations.

Emotional growth requires purposeful, emotional intelligence development. Psychologists Peter Salovey and John Mayer defined emotional intelligence as recognizing, comprehending, managing, and controlling emotions in oneself and others. These skills include self-awareness, self-regulation, social awareness, and relationship management. High-EQ people handle human interactions with empathy, resilience, and good communication, improving personal and societal well-being.

Continuous emotional growth involves challenges and setbacks. Personal failures, grief, and unexpected changes test emotional resilience. Face problems with courage, adaptability, and a growth mentality to show emotional maturity. Emotionally growing people see setbacks as opportunities to learn, self-discover, and improve coping skills.

Mindfulness activities like meditation and self-reflection aid emotional growth. A non-judgmental awareness of the current moment allows people to view their thoughts and feelings without attachment. These routines improve self-awareness, emotional regulation, and intelligent response. Mindfulness helps build resilience and calmness in life's unavoidable hardships.

Accepting vulnerability helps emotional growth. Acknowledging and expressing one's true feelings takes courage in a culture that views vulnerability as weakness. Brene Brown, a researcher and storyteller, says vulnerability fosters connection, creativity, and resilience. Vulnerability helps people connect more truthfully and grow emotionally by exposing them to human experience.

Developing a growth mindset is crucial to emotional growth. A growth mindset, coined by psychologist Carol S. Dweck, holds that effort, study, and perseverance may improve intelligence and abilities. Growth-minded people are curious about challenges and see failures as learning opportunities. This perspective fosters emotional resilience and healthy, adaptive personal development.

Emotional growth occurs in families, communities, and cultures. Culture and society's views on emotional expression, mental health, and vulnerability affect people's emotional development. Creating supportive workplaces that destigmatize mental health, encourage open communication, and prioritize emotional well-being helps us grow and thrive.

In conclusion, emotional growth is a lifetime process that requires self-awareness, life experiences, relationships, deliberate practices, vulnerability, and a growth mentality. Accepting emotions, learning from obstacles, and actively fostering emotional intelligence improves personal and collective well-being. Individuals' unique and everyday journeys through their dynamic landscapes impact their own growth and the growth of their communities and cultures.

CONCLUSION

In conclusion, "Emotional Alchemy: Transforming Feelings into Personal Growth - A Practical Handbook for Emotional Intelligence" is a beacon of insight and guidance in emotional well-being. Through its thoughtful investigation of dynamic alchemy, the book invites readers on a transforming journey where feelings are not barriers but chances for personal progress. The theoretical foundations of emotional intelligence are made sure to be more than just notions to be comprehended; instead, they are instruments to be applied in the real-world complexities of life through the practical handbook approach.

The book's essence is encapsulated in the title,

"Emotional Alchemy," which transforms the essential components of our emotions into something valuable and changing. Its subtitle, "A Practical Handbook for Emotional Intelligence, " further highlights the book's practical approach," which provides concrete methods and activities to improve emotional intelligence in day-to-day situations.

The author expertly combines psychological insights,

true stories, and doable actions across the pages to provide readers with a thorough manual for navigating the complex terrain of emotions. Whether exploring the subtleties of self-awareness, interpersonal dynamics, or resilience building, the book offers a path for transforming emotional setbacks into learning experiences.

"Emotional Alchemy" is vital not just because of its

theoretical underpinnings but also because of its practicality in various real situations. Through the book's presentation of emotional intelligence as a valuable skill set, readers can set out on their emotional alchemical journey and turn obstacles into opportunities for personal growth. Readers are encouraged to actively incorporate emotional intelligence into their lives and comprehend them as they interact with the material.

"Emotional Alchemy" appears as a relevant and priceless resource in a society where mental health is becoming more widely acknowledged as a foundation of general health. It gives readers the skills they need to work through the intricacies of their own emotions and pave the way for long-term personal development, deeper connections, and more self-awareness. This book invites readers to embark on a journey towards emotional mastery and, eventually, a more robust and rewarding existence. It is not just a book to be read; it is an experiential guide.

Thank you for buying and reading/ listening to our book. If you found this book useful/ helpful please take a few minutes and leave a review on the platform where you purchased our book. Your feedback matters greatly to us.

www.ingramcontent.com/pod-product-compliance
Lightning Source LLC
Chambersburg PA
CBHW052045150726
48002CB00002B/760